Teaching Reading in High School English Classes

Teaching Reading in High School English Classes

Edited by

Bonnie O. Ericson
California State University, Northridge

National Council of Teachers of English
1111 W. Kenyon Road, Urbana, IL 61801-1096

We gratefully acknowledge Kane/Miller Book Publishers, who generously gave us permission to reproduce the cover of *Wilfrid Gordon McDonald Partridge* by Mem Fox, Illustrated by Julie Vivas. First American edition published in 1985 by Kane/Miller Book Publishers, Brooklyn, New York. Originally published in Australia in 1984 by Omnibus Books. Text copyright © 1984 Mem Fox. Illustrations copyright © 1984 Julie Vivas.

Staff Editor: Bonny Graham

Interior Design: Doug Burnett

Cover Design: Tom Jaczak

Cover Photos: Elizabeth Crews

NCTE Stock Number: 51868-3050

©2001 by the National Council of Teachers of English.

Library of Congress Cataloging-in-Publication Data

Teaching reading in high school English classes / edited by Bonnie O. Ericson.
     p. cm.
   "NCTE stock number: 51868-3050."
   Includes bibliographical references.
   ISBN 0-8141-5186-8 (pbk.)
    1. Reading (Secondary)—United States.   2. Literature—Study and teaching (Secondary)—United States.   I. Ericson, Bonnie O.

LB1632 .T37   2001
428.4′071′2–dc21

                                           2001045235

This book is dedicated to my parents, Robert and Dorothy Ohrlund, to my husband, Dan Blake, and to all the teachers who make a difference in the reading lives of their students.

Use chapter 4, 5 +1
in my struggling sts
Course

8 + Chapter 6
Also have Jenifer Wolf
come + talk about chapter
9 and bring YA Books
applicable across
the curriculum

Hilton
Washington Embassy Row

2015 Massachusetts Ave., N.W.
Washington, DC 20036
Telephone 202 265 1600
Fax 202 328 7526
Reservations: www.hilton.com
or 1 800 HILTONS

Foreword: Welcome to the Planet of the Readers

John S. Mayher
New York University

W hen I started teaching high school in ancient times, I suddenly found myself confronted by students from another planet. I was from the planet of the readers, and it was soon clear to me that with few exceptions, they were not. It wasn't that I had never known such aliens before; I'd gone to school with a few of them, and as an elementary and secondary student, even my brother seemed to have had such alien blood. But roomful after roomful of them was a shock, and certainly something neither my experience nor my education had prepared me for.

I had been a reader from as far back as I could remember, and there was no time when I wasn't reading at least one, and often two or more books at the same time. Many of my happiest hours throughout my childhood and adolescence were spent reading, and I often sought out reading time in preference to other forms of recreation. Where else, after all, could one visit remote places and, particularly, remote times except in a story? And, even more important, how else could one live lives other than one's own? Or learn how to live the one life we have? In my generation, there were few alternatives to books as places to find these stories. And there were no other places where one could find the stories on demand.

The need for narrative is one of the strongest human needs, and indeed Mark Turner (1996) has argued that we have what he calls a literary mind, which is, in his view, the source of our language and our grammar. James Britton used to argue that our need for story started with gossip and moved deeper and more complexly into other genres without completely leaving the voyeurism and moral judgments of gossip behind (1982). This need, of course, has not left kids at all. They are more in touch with each other than any generation ever has been: beepers with voice mail, cell phones, answering machines, call waiting, and their own phone lines. I'll never forget the moment I watched my teenage daughter talking on two phone lines, a phone at each ear, while simultaneously writing to both of the people she was talking to and others in an AOL chat room—the radio, of course, providing a soundtrack of teenage laments.

The need for narrative has not disappeared, but the competition for reading as a source of story has become much more intense. Television is in color, not black and white, and there are a hundred or more channels available to virtually every adolescent in the United States. Many kids even have their own TV set, and, as often as not, continual access to a VCR—not even a dream in 1962 when I began teaching— which they fully understand how to program. Radio is still with us—in some ways the least changed of the media for teens—as are movies aimed directly at the teen audience. An additional range of entertainment options comes with the computer and the Internet for those able to avail themselves of them. The new millennium is awash in a kid culture the likes of which the world has never seen.

When, as a beginning teacher, I first met these aliens from the nonreading planet, it took me a while to adjust to the world my students were living in and the nature of their reading (or, mostly, nonreading) experiences, but I found that many of them could be, in Dan Fader's memorable phrase, "hooked on books" (Fader & McNeil, 1968). In that era, the books were usually more "real" than the equivalent TV shows and movies, and that helped them speak to the kids of the sixties and seventies. The books needed to be relevant to them, and many of us discovered and helped promote the distribution of books specifically written for young adults. We searched for and found books written for adults but that spoke to the issues of development that teenagers were facing. Some of these have become near classics today, such as *The Catcher in the Rye*, *A Separate Peace*, and *To Kill a Mockingbird*.

And so, as a more and more sophisticated group of YA writers developed their talents, there were more and more YA books available for kids to find. At the same time, however, television and movies shucked their *Ozzie and Harriet* or *Father Knows Best* rosy glow and began to speak more directly to kids as well. By the eighties and certainly in the nineties, adolescents had an enormous range of narrative alternatives to satisfy their need for story.

What's a poor English teacher to do?

This volume hopes to provide some answers to this question, and to help teachers help twenty-first-century young adults find joy in reading. That's the key for me: the experience of being enraptured by a story that takes us beyond the life we are living.

For this to happen, a delicate balance of skill and interest is crucial, since if one doesn't read well enough—fast enough, fluently enough, powerfully enough—the frustrations will overwhelm any possible pleasure to be gained from being interested in the story. Because there are no shortcuts here, the only way to develop the necessary skills is by "doing the thing itself"—by reading, reading, reading, and then by talking, talking, talking about the experience. Frank Smith characterizes the learning process involved as *Joining the Literacy Club* (1988), although for adolescents it's more like rejoining since for many it's a question of reconnecting to the possibilities of written texts. They were often most connected to written stories when they were read to as children, if they were lucky enough to have had those experiences.

Indeed, the notion of a book club may provide one model of the kind of mutual support system necessary to get reluctant readers involved. Certainly it works for adults, and one of the essential elements of a successful middle or high school reading program is powerful evidence that the adults who are working with kids are themselves active readers. Preaching the virtues of reading has little effect if the preachers are not weekly arriving in classrooms with stories of how much they are enjoying *Angela's Ashes* or *The Bean Trees* or *Jazz*. If we as teachers are not living models of the power and joys of reading, it will be impossible for our charges to take us seriously.

Most important, we must understand that helping all of the students in our classes become better readers is our responsibility. Reading is not something that one learns to do once in elementary school; it is a lifelong process of growth as one meets the challenges of new texts. When we signed on to be English teachers, many of us thought that "teaching reading" was something someone else did. Some kids may need additional support beyond practice and sharing, and teachers must be alert for signs of more severe dysfunction. Some of these students may need more specialized support than we can provide, but even as we seek out help for them, we have to recognize that the basic process of making it possible for kids to succeed at reading a book they enjoy is a fundamental part of our job.

Sadly, in many if not most of our classes there will be kids who have never read a book voluntarily, as well as others who have never finished any book, even those they have been "required" to read. And saddest of all, there will be some who were never read to as children. So whether we are dealing with kids who can read but don't, or those who don't read because they are fearful of doing so, our goal should be to enable kids to have enough positive, involving experiences with written stories that they will continue to seek them out long after they have left us. It is probably too much to expect to turn them into print addicts like me, but every kid who responds to the call of stories through our intervention and support will be grateful to us throughout their lives. Those of us who live on the planet of the readers will be equally grateful for their company.

References

Britton, J. (1982). *Prospect and retrospect: Selected essays of James Britton*. (G. Pradl, Ed.) Portsmouth, NH: Boynton/Cook.

Fader, D., & McNeil, E. (1968). *Hooked on books: Program and proof*. New York: Putnam.

Smith, F. (1988). *Joining the literacy club: Further essays into education*. Portsmouth, NH: Heinemann.

Turner, M. (1996). *The literary mind*. Oxford: Oxford University Press.

Preface

Most high school English teachers consider themselves teachers of literature, teachers of composition, teachers of language. But reading teachers? One of the main purposes of this book is to reassure high school English teachers that they already know a great deal about the teaching of reading, and that in fact most are already teaching reading every day as they provide activities that foster a love of reading or guide discussions on vocabulary, make inferences about character or setting, and allow students to make connections to personal experiences. But as is always the case with teaching, more can be done.

How is it that we find ourselves at this juncture where reading and English sometimes seem to occupy wholly different realms? The answer is largely in the histories of the two fields. The instruction involved with learning to read and remedial reading, often accomplished by our colleagues in the primary and later elementary grades, as well as the professional literature base for beginning and remedial reading, grew originally from the field of psychology. The teaching of literature and its professional research base claim entirely different roots in philosophy. But over the past century, as reading grew "up" to include reading instruction at all levels and as literature instruction moved "down" to elementary levels, clashes of understanding have sometimes occurred because professionals in these two areas often speak different languages and hold different assumptions.

Yet here at the beginning of the twenty-first century, the different ability levels and backgrounds of our students—mainstreamed students with text processing difficulties, recent immigrants with limited education in a first language, those with high SAT scores aspiring to attend prestigious universities, students diagnosed with ADHD, and all the others who attend our classes—make it obvious that the reading needs in high school English classrooms are incredibly varied. The good news is that we do know a tremendous amount about teaching reading in high school English. And we do agree on the goal of producing fluent and engaged readers, students whose lives are enriched by reading, students whose choices in life are expanded by their reading capabilities.

To that end, the chapters in *Teaching Reading in High School English Classes* taken together promote what is called a "balanced" approach to reading. That is, readers, including those at the high school level, have varying needs for reading instruction. Most students, even those in Advanced Placement English classes, require instruction and opportunities to further develop their comprehension capabilities. Many students, including those who read "at grade level," need more extensive practice or experience with reading in order to develop greater reading fluency. Some portion of our students at the high school level, for a wide array of reasons, also requires some assistance with decoding. Many students will benefit from instruction and opportunities in *all* these areas. Although addressing the reading needs of students is a responsibility shared across the subject areas, it is English teachers who are most often called on. And so the chapters in this book describe successful practices and programs of reading instruction for high school English classrooms.

John Mayher's foreword reminds us of the key role narrative plays in the lives of all humans, including adolescents, and suggests that perhaps our primary responsibility as English teachers is to find ways for our students to discover the joys of reading. Chapter 1 provides an overview of what reading entails and various approaches to reading instruction in high school English classes. In Chapter 2, Janet S. Allen highlights a key component of reading, vocabulary, and gives examples of successful vocabulary activities for adolescents.

The next four chapters focus on reading instruction for students who struggle with reading. John Gaughan's thought-provoking chapter advises English teachers to use contemporary and multicultural literature, selections that speak most directly to students and their life experiences. Gaughan also demonstrates the power of making connections between reading and writing assignments. In Chapter 4, Linda L. Flammer explains a balanced reading intervention program for ninth graders who are predominantly from Spanish-speaking backgrounds, a program that has allowed students to achieve success throughout their high school years. Susan Schauwecker outlines the components of her reading class for seniors from both English and English language learner (ELL) backgrounds who must pass a basic skills examination in order to graduate from high school. And, in Chapter 6, Jeff McQuillan and a group of high school teachers describe the logistics and outcomes of a highly successful sustained silent reading program for struggling readers at their urban high school.

Sandra Okura DaLie explains in Chapter 7 how she has incorporated literature circles as a valued component of teaching across grade and ability levels in her high school English classes, and in Chapter 8 Teri S. Lesesne and Lois Buckman promote practices to help capable but reluctant readers rediscover the satisfactions of reading. Lesesne and Buckman's work exhorts us to find ways to make reading valued and meaningful for all readers.

The final chapters concentrate on two types of literature often overlooked in grades 9 through 12. Lois T. Stover's chapter defines young adult literature, delineates types of YA literature, and describes ways this literature can increase the competence of high school readers, while in Chapter 10 Carolyn Lott brings children's literature to the high school classroom through creative teaching ideas and reading selections ranging from the powerful to the charming. Finally, in her afterword, Leila Christenbury celebrates the value of reading and urges English teachers to agree on several core propositions as a way to ensure a promising future of reading for all adolescents.

These chapters bring together information and examples about what high-quality, balanced reading instruction entails. Most high school English teachers will see themselves in some of these chapters; they will most certainly also encounter new practices that they may adopt for use in their classes. It's time that all high school English teachers address reading in their classrooms. *Teaching Reading in High School English Classes* is an attempt to point the way.

Bonnie O. Ericson

Acknowledgments

Thanks first and foremost go to the chapter authors who contributed and persevered as the book made its way to publication. I am also grateful to Pete Feely, Bonny Graham, and the NCTE Editorial Board for their helpful advice and suggestions. Finally, thanks go to two English education M.A. cohorts at my university, both for their insightful commentary about individual chapters and for the inspiration they provided in sharing their teaching stories.

1 Reading in High School English Classes: An Overview

Bonnie O. Ericson
California State University, Northridge

A tremendous amount of public attention has recently been focused on the reading abilities—or disabilities—of U.S. students. From the National Assessment of Educational Progress (NAEP) reports that 40 percent of U.S. fourth graders read below grade level, to the National Council of Teachers of English's Reading Initiative (Harris, 1999), reading is news. Much of this attention addresses beginning reading and reading in the early to middle elementary years. At that level, the so-called reading wars over the best early literacy instructional practices are alive and well, despite numerous voices calling for balance and moderation.

High school English teachers, however, are traditionally viewed—and view themselves—as outside the teaching of reading, because the assumption has been that students come to them knowing how to read. High school English teachers see themselves primarily as teachers of literature and composition and grammar. Yet, whenever a group of high school English teachers meets, they are likely to voice concern over their students' lack of reading skills, even those of the more able students. And certainly they pose questions about the number of students who seem to lack the most fundamental of reading skills.

The literacy of our youth is indeed a critical issue in society and in education, all the more so because increasingly higher literacy skills are required to function successfully in society. Miles Myers (1996) convincingly describes how literacy demands have evolved over historical periods, from the oral literacy of the 1600s to the literacy of "decoding, defining, and analyzing" of the 1900s. In the early years of the new millennium, literacy demands continue to increase. According to Myers, the newest standard of literacy calls for students to interpret and solve problems in reading and writing. At the same time, the high school graduation rate has climbed steadily in the past one hundred years; in 1900 the high school graduation rate was about 3 percent, and not until the 1950s was it above 50 percent (Bracey, 1977). Currently, over 80 per-cent of the population graduates from high school (Bracey, 1997). A focus on academic standards is one outgrowth of the combination of increased literacy needs and greater numbers of students from all backgrounds staying in school.

Through academic content standards, various groups hope to ensure higher student achievement and greater teacher accountability. State or district standards are those with which teachers are most fa-miliar, but the National Council of Teachers of English (NCTE) and the International Reading Association (IRA) also co-developed and adopted a set of national standards for all grade levels, the first three of which address reading:

> 3. Students apply a wide range of strategies to comprehend, interpret, evaluate, and appreciate texts. They draw on their prior experience, their interactions with other readers and writ-ers, their knowledge of word meaning and of other texts, their word identification strategies, and their understanding of tex-tual features (e.g., sound-letter correspondence, sentence struc-ture, context, graphics). (1996, p. 3)

As the standards movement calls for higher levels of reading profi-ciency, students come to high school English classes with a tremendous range of reading abilities. High school En-glish teachers rarely have the backgrounds to assist the least able readers in their classes, and additionally are often uncer-tain about what reading instruction actu-ally involves. What are these "wide range of strategies" referred to in the NCTE/IRA standards? How can English teachers ad-dress the curriculum and teach reading, too? Doesn't a focus on reading just get in the way of reading and discussing litera-ture? This chapter attempts to address these questions and to clarify what a balanced approach to the teaching of reading means for high school English teachers, while providing a framework for later chapters.

High school English teachers rarely have the backgrounds to assist the least able readers in their classes, and additionally are often uncertain about what reading instruction actually involves.

The Reading Process

It has been my experience that high school students think they are ei-ther good readers or poor readers, and that there's little in between. When asked what it means to be a good reader, they might simply ex-

Hilton

Washington Embassy Row

2015 Massachusetts Ave., N.W.
Washington, DC 20036
Telephone 202 265 1600
Fax 202 328 7526
Reservations: www.hilton.com
or 1 800 HILTONS

plain that good readers are fast readers or that good readers find it easy to read all the words and answer questions about the reading. Or they may believe that good readers make few mistakes when reading aloud in class. These explanations fail to account for the complexity and developmental nature of the reading process. Perhaps one of our tasks as English teachers is to help students see some of this complexity with reading, much as we have addressed the complexity of writing with writing process instruction. Many literacy experts believe that an interactive model of the reading process best captures how most students at the high school level read:

> They connect what they know about language, decoding, and vocabulary to their background experiences and prior knowledge. They also take into account the demands of the reading task and reasons for which they are reading. However, [readers run into trouble] when decoding is not automatic or when insufficient prior knowledge prevents readers from conceptually making sense of print. (Alvermann & Phelps, 1998, 24)

Most of us would add that readers are likely to have problems if they are not motivated or if they have a history of reading failure. But this definition of the reading process, however accurate, sounds remarkably foreign to us, and in fact probably leaves us cold. That's because there is no mention of the joy of reading—the wonder of living in another time, experiencing the life of a person completely unlike anyone we know, or following an eloquent argument. What we need to do is consider both issues: whether our students experience the "magic" of reading is influenced by the difficulty of a reading selection; their motivation; their background knowledge, prior experiences, and interest in a reading selection; the classroom and home cultures; the purpose(s) for reading; their vocabulary knowledge; their sight word and decoding abilities; their English-language facility; and the presence or lack of learning disabilities (Alvermann & Phelps, 1998; Readence, Bean, & Baldwin, 1995). We English teachers can bring the magic of reading to our students best when we are aware of the potential roadblocks presented by these factors, remembering that some factors we can influence, some we can control, and others we must simply take into account.

Another important aspect of the reading process recognized by reading specialists is metacognition, or the awareness and monitoring of one's thinking processes. When applied to reading, metacognition

means that readers know when they are understanding and when
they are not, and they know when they are making connections—if
they are "into" the reading, if they value the reading. Further,
metacognition involves knowing ways to fix a problem with reading,
perhaps by rereading or slowing the pace of reading, or, in some cases,
by making a change of reading selection. "Metacognition" isn't a term
we utter frequently, but we are concerned with it nevertheless. English
teachers are reading teachers when we attend to metacognitive factors
and when we promote the values of reading literature and other materials. We are reading teachers when we provide instruction and experiences that encourage students to be active makers of meaning in
their reading.

Approaches to Reading
for High School English Classes

For students to continue to grow in their reading abilities at the high
school level and to see reading as a meaningful activity, we need to
implement a variety of approaches. Among those often viewed as
central are guided reading, independent reading, group reading,
and reading aloud. Again, we English teachers may be unaccus-
tomed to articulating our practices in this way, but these approaches
are familiar.

Guided Reading

In guided reading, a class reads a challenging selection with teacher
guidance or teacher-structured activities before, during, and after reading. English teachers use the "into, through, and beyond" terminology,
another way of describing guided reading. The fact that a teacher is
guiding instruction, however, does not mean that students are at the
periphery of learning. Parallels to the writing process help explain
guided reading. In writing process instruction, prewriting activities
help students generate and organize ideas for writing. Prereading
("into") activities fill a similar function for the reading process: they
draw out what students already know and think about authors or issues in the reading. In drafting, students produce a first written attempt at what they wish to communicate in their writing. Similarly,
during-reading ("through") activities ask students to construct an initial understanding of their reading. Peer response to a written draft
and the revision of a draft correspond to postreading ("beyond") instruction, follow-up efforts to gain additional insights about a reading

Approaches to Reading that can be adapted to Other Content Areas

, guided reading is recursive or
-by-step process.

with prereading activities such as
er successful prereading technique
debatable statements topically con-
y (e.g., Parents always know what
ly justifiable). Students respond to
in a class or group discussion. Yet
prereading activity involves select-
rips of paper a number of key quo-
e numbered according to the order
ll groups of students can each be
hen discuss what the lines might
to the quotation. Quickly and se-
loud so that the class hears all the
e selection can be discussed.

rest for reading, prereading activi-
ounds about a subject by defining
oviding pronunciations of proper
k of Amontillado," students might
ge and, depending on the group,
ng "Montresor," "Fortunato," and

of guided reading, students read
se of it. Teachers may ask students
ssign a section for homework or
ay read in small groups, or they
a readers' theater approach (stu-
), either as a whole class or in
aning by visualizing, confirming,
uestions; completing quickwrites;
t clearly understood. If students
erline, highlight, or write notes in
the margins. Even when schools own the books, Post-it notes can be
used for writing responses. During-reading instruction also involves
initial responses to reading such as writing log entries, discussing as a
class, completing graphic organizers, or writing answers to questions.
At this time, students are focusing on a basic understanding of the
material.

Finally, in postreading activities students reassess and broaden
their understandings, extending and perhaps revising earlier thoughts.

They may focus on how a character has changed over the duration of a novel, or how setting has influenced understanding of the story. Similarly, symbolic understandings or emotional reactions may be revisited, the author's language choices evaluated, or a video version viewed for purposes of comparison and contrast. Here, the focus is on appreciation, interpretation, evaluation, and an understanding of human nature, life, the world. English teachers may have students engage in genuine and meaningful discussion, assume the persona of a character to write a letter or journal entry in the character's voice, create and perform a scene that did not appear in the book, or, yes, write an analytical essay. "Beyond" activities ask students to stretch their understandings, and the classroom culture becomes key to the success of these activities.

A guided reading strategy that several recent student teachers found valuable is called K-W-L (Carr & Ogle, 1987; Ogle, 1986). Before reading, students list what they *k*now about a topic related to the reading. Then they list what they *w*ant to know, often in the form of questions. Following reading, they reexamine what they wanted to know, then list what they *l*earned from the reading. This activity is particularly effective when focused on characters following the reading of several chapters in a full-length work or on plot near the end of a work, although K-W-L is effective with expository or informational pieces as well.

A guided reading approach is an attempt to genuinely motivate students, prepare them for reading, work through a selection, and come to understandings of and judgments about characters, situations, themes, and language—and how all these connect. The extent to which guided reading activities are planned depends on how challenging the text is and how much support will benefit students. For instance, "sheltered" instruction for classes just gaining fluency in English is marked by a large number of guided reading activities. Guided reading, however, is only one of several reading approaches for high school English classes.

Independent Reading

Another crucial approach to reading instruction for high school English classes is independent reading. For independent reading, students usually choose their own reading selections, and there are no (or at least very limited) prereading activities, vocabulary notebooks, or comprehension questions. Students simply begin at the beginning of a work and proceed on their own. Independent reading selections should be accessible to students, either because the student is genuinely interested in and motivated to read or because the work poses fewer reading challenges. High school students often choose popular adult fiction—mysteries, romance, science fiction—or young adult literature (see Stover, Chapter 9 of this volume) for independent reading. Teachers or school and public librarians may recommend selections or provide several choices, but in the end the actual selection is left to the student. Students are on their own during reading and the process of making sense of a work.

How do we encourage independent reading? Some high schools have a schoolwide time for SSR (sustained, silent reading, or, as one of my daughters once explained to me, "sit down, shut up, and read"). Teachers may provide independent reading time for ten to fifteen minutes at the beginning of class a couple of days a week or every day during a particular unit. They may also structure their grading so that independent reading is rewarded. Whether this is achieved by requiring a certain number of books or by assigning extra credit points, such systems send a powerful message concerning the importance of reading.

Reading workshop approaches for middle school students have been described by Atwell (1998) and modified for the high school level. In reading workshop, the teacher typically begins class with a short lesson that addresses student needs or the required curriculum. Mini-lesson topics might include information on and discussion about particular authors, genres, literary elements, effective titles or story beginnings, types of characters, and the like. Students then engage in one or more reading activities for the bulk of the reading workshop time: silent reading, writing a brief response, conferencing with peers or the teacher. The workshop closes with a quick sharing of what each student has accomplished that day. Key elements of reading workshop are reading choice, active student involvement and responsibility, a reading workshop portfolio, and teacher record keeping. High school teachers, after some initial explanation and modeling for students, may use reading workshop as a several-week unit during each semester, or use one or two days a week for the semester as reading workshop days.

Promoting independent reading, whether through SSR or reading workshop, requires a literacy-rich classroom environment, including classroom libraries of appealing and appropriate titles so that students have ready access to a great variety of reading materials. A literacy-rich environment might entail regular visits by the school librarian to promote new acquisitions, or posters—either commercial or student created—on the walls featuring books or authors. And a literacy-rich environment would most certainly be enhanced by teachers who share their own reading, even if only through a thirty-second summary of a book just begun or the reading aloud of one or two paragraphs that were especially compelling from an article in yesterday's newspaper. Students need reading models, and as English teachers we have both a responsibility and a wonderful opportunity to share our own reading.

Independent reading is a critical element of a strong reading program at the high school level. For the myriad reasons we can all recite, today's students too rarely have or make time for independent reading. Jobs, assigned reading and homework, activities with friends, and cable television and the Internet all vie for their time outside of school. But unless students have the opportunity to practice reading, experience success and pleasure with reading, and have the freedom to make their own reading choices, we may well lose them as readers. Some may be capable readers but choose not to read, the so-called aliterates, but others' abilities will falter through lack of practice. For the readers already struggling with reading, this lack of independent reading may well contribute to future illiteracy. Independent reading corresponds to various types of "fluency" writing, such as journal writing or quick-writes. The point is to practice in a risk-free environment; this practice in turn builds fluency and a positive attitude (see McQuillan et al., Chapter 6 of this volume).

Literature Circles and Other Forms of Group Reading

Somewhere between guided and independent reading falls group reading. One of the most valuable of the group reading approaches is literature circles (Daniels, 1994; DaLie, Chapter 7 of this volume):

> Literature circles are small, temporary discussion groups who have chosen to read the same story, poem, article, or book. While reading each group-determined portion of the text (either in or outside of class), each member prepares to take specific responsibilities in the upcoming discussion, and everyone comes to the group with the notes needed to help perform that job. The circles have regular meetings, with discussion roles rotating each session. When they finish a book, the circle members plan a way to share highlights of their reading with the wider community; then they trade members with other finishing groups, select more reading, and move into a new cycle. Once readers can successfully conduct their own wide-ranging, self-sustaining discussions, formal discussion roles may be dropped. (Daniels, 1994, p. 13)

In providing literature circle selections, high school teachers sometimes limit the choices of texts, often to a number of selections related thematically in some way. One colleague presents a series of eight books, each set in a different decade beginning with the 1920s, and groups are formed from individuals' choices of decade. Some teachers run literature circles during the reading of a core work, thereby extending the total time that a literature unit runs but encouraging connections between the core and group works.

Apart from literature circles, group reading might also be regularly implemented in high school English classrooms by asking groups to read and respond to different selections or having groups all read the same short selection and then compare their understandings and responses with other groups in the class.

Why should group reading be included in a program of reading? One reason is that this form of reading builds independence from the teacher and allows students to practice important reading skills. More important, however, is the chance for students to share the pleasure of reading, talking, and arguing with their peers in ways similar to their discussions about movies or television programs. Again, we send a message about what is important when we give it time in our classrooms for students of all abilities.

Reading Aloud

A final form reading takes in high school English classes is reading aloud, although not the round-robin version we may recall from our elementary school years. Usually, the teacher or a capable student reads aloud (or perhaps is heard on tape) with effective voice inflections and energy, pauses, and even sound effects. Most good readers had the experience of being read to when they were young, and so they developed notions of narrative and early literacy skills (turning the pages, words on the page have meaning, reading from left to right and from the top of the page to the bottom, etc.). Snuggled close to a parent, relative, or other caretaker, these children also established early, positive attitudes to reading. Unfortunately, not all sixteen-year-olds were read to as young children. The pleasurable experience of listening to someone else read helps establish or recapture these positive attitudes to reading and story. Additionally, those students who come from families in which English is not the first language benefit from hearing a fluent reader. Other students may simply appreciate some time to sit back and enjoy the power of language and story.

Two additional forms of reading aloud include readers' theater performances and choral reading. Asking students to engage in reading aloud to others, whether their classmates, younger students, or the elderly, requires students to reread a selection multiple times. The results? Development of reading fluency, promotion of the idea that understandings of and responses to a work evolve, and a sense of satisfaction from performing for an audience. With service learning proposed in many communities as a high school graduation requirement, reading aloud may yet become a more common practice. Both aspects—being read aloud to and reading aloud to others—have value.

All of the approaches described—guided reading, independent reading, group reading, and reading aloud—contribute to a total reading program in the English classroom at the high school level. Providing experiences in all these approaches will make a difference in student reading.

Reading Selections for High School English

Variety, variety, variety. No matter the classroom approach, the value of offering a variety of types and levels of selections for reading simply cannot be overstated. Most of us have found ways to build a small classroom library of novels, and most of us have access to literature anthologies and other paperbacks or hardbacks of single titles in a textbook room. But I would suggest several important additions, to be acquired through special purchase funds or through loans from school or public libraries. (Some of you are perhaps guilty of making personal purchases for classroom use.) Whatever the source, and in addition to the usual selections, students need ready access to collections of poetry, essays, and short stories; multicultural literature; contemporary fiction; young adult and children's literature; magazines and newspapers; and informational texts and nonfiction works. To limit our selections to novels, especially to the "classic" novels, is to tell our students that all these other texts, perhaps the students' preferred types of reading, have less value. And to limit class reading to novels, especially to the classic novels, is to limit students' bridges to the joy of reading. The paragraphs below address poetry and essays, two forms of literature sometimes neglected in high school class libraries.

The reading of poetry calls for a particular type of reading, in part because of the concise form and the attention poets give to the sounds and rhythm of the language they choose. Too often, however, students' reading experiences with poetic language are limited. While the Internet is a new source of poetry for teachers and students, numerous poetry collections with appeal to high school students are readily available. *Cool Salsa: Bilingual Poems on Growing Up Latino in the United States* (Carlson, 1994) is a collection with both English and Spanish versions of the same poem. In *The Language of Life: A Festival of Poets* (1995), Bill Moyers presents transcripts of interviews with contemporary poets, along with several of their powerful poems. *Poetspeak: In Their Work, about Their Work* (Janeczko, 1983) also offers contemporary poetry, along with the poets' comments on their work. Fleischmann's *Joyful Noise: Poems for Two Voices* (1988) is a delightful collection of poems about insects and other creatures that are excellent choices for choral reading. For many years a favorite, *Reflections on a Gift of Watermelon Pickle and Other Modern Verse* has been updated and expanded (Dunning, Leuders, Nye, Gilyard, & Worley, 1995).

To promote independent reading of poetry, one colleague has her students create their own books of selected poems, copying favorites from independent reading and perhaps including original poems as well. Another teacher friend displays a poem a day on the overhead projector at the beginning of the class period. Her students read and respond in their poetry logs to the poem and then share some of their insights and connections in a brief whole-class discussion. After several weeks, she moves on to another type of class-opening activity. Since these are hardly new ideas, English teachers should be aware that these are reading activities.

Essays are another specific type of reading students need to experience regularly in their English classes. Because students are or should be asked to write different types of essays, we need to be certain they read a variety of types of essays, with opportunities to consider essay structures, arguments, and rhetorical devices. Claggett (1996) describes four main types of essays for classroom reading and writing: expressive (autobiographical writing, biographical sketches, and the reflective essay), informative (report of information and observational essays), persuasive (problem-solution, evaluation, speculation, interpretation, and controversial issue), and literary (any of the others at a sophisticated level). High school students should be exposed to all these types, which isn't difficult because they are surrounded by essays in daily newspapers (including the sports section), all kinds of magazines, Internet Web sites, and collections readily available in public libraries and bookstores. Recommended contemporary writers with published collections of essays or works easily found in other collections include Julia Alvarez, Erma Bombeck, Bill Cosby, Ellen Goodman, Barbara Kingsolver, Barry Lopez, Gerald Haslam, Rudolfo Anaya, Russell Baker, and Andres Dubus.

Essays often can be incorporated in high school classes as thematically related reading selections to inform and supplement the reading of fiction or biographical writing. The colleague who uses poetry reading and responding for a class-opening activity might use essay reading and responding in the same way. Pairs of essays that address similar topics can be presented and evaluated for their effectiveness. Jigsaw group reading (Vacca & Vacca, 1999) of different essays might also be carried out in high school English classes.

One of my favorite essays for guided reading is Andres Dubus's "Woman in April," a sophisticated piece for juniors or seniors (Haynes & Landsman, 1998). In teaching this autobiographical essay, I use the prereading activity with quotations described earlier, presenting ten quotations to groups of students, including these two: "She angled back to her first path, as though it were painted there for her to follow, and Philip said: 'That *never* happens in New York'" (p. 81) and "Living in the world as a cripple allows you to see more clearly the crippled hearts of some people whose bodies are whole and sound" (p. 81). Student discussion has been filled with remarkable comments and questions that have led to insightful readings and eventually to compelling writings.

Persuasive essays are commonly published in newspapers and frequently lend themselves to response in the form of a diagram. After an initial reading of a persuasive piece, students determine a central yes/no question addressed in the essay (e.g., Should the press write about government officials' personal lives? Should the term 'African American' be changed to 'Black American'?). Placing this central question in a circle on a piece of paper, they then reread the essay and list reasons supporting a no answer to the left of the circle and reasons supporting a yes answer to the right of the circle. A discussion about the persuasiveness of the reasons can ensue, followed by students drawing their own conclusions to the central question posed in the essay. Again, this activity can be considered an example of reading instruction because it focuses on a central idea and asks for supporting evidence and evaluation of that evidence.

Clagget, Reid, and Vinz (1999) have edited a series called *Daybook of Critical Reading and Writing* for students in grades 6 through 12. These remarkable collections belong on the shelves of all high school

English teachers, if not in the backpacks of their students, because they include an outstanding collection of short pieces, including poetry and essays, as well as accompanying activities that facilitate the development of reading in a variety of genres.

In addition to poetry and essays, multicultural literature clearly has a place in classroom reading and libraries no matter who the students are. Incorporating multicultural literacy isn't merely "politically correct," as some would have it; rather, multicultural works display high literary merit and promote examination of important social and cultural issues. At times, guided reading may help students better understand cultural differences and similarities, as well as written language dialects or historically relevant information. Other times, students may choose multicultural works for independent or group reading. Multicultural selections that have been used successfully at the high school level (Ericson, 1997) include, among many possibilities, *Parrot in the Oven* (Martinez); *The House on Mango Street* (Cisneros); *Bless Me, Ultima* (Anaya); *Shabanu, Daughter of the Wind* (Staples); *Nectar in a Sieve* (Markandaya); *I Know Why the Caged Bird Sings* (Angelou); *Fallen Angels* (Myers); *Their Eyes Were Watching God* (Hurston); *Make Lemonade* (Wolff); *Children of the River* (Crew); and *The Joy Luck Club* (Tan). Excellent short story collections are *The Loom and Other Stories*; *A Gathering of Flowers: Stories about Being Young in America* (Thomas) and *Join In: Multiethnic Short Stories by Outstanding Writers for Young Adults* (Gallo).

Levels and Types of Reading

In their attempts to get a better handle on reading, reading specialists and literacy response theorists have described levels or types of reading skills, comprehension, and response. High school English teachers are probably aware of some of these designations, but a quick review is in order because of the direct implications these have for class activities and student assessment. If, for example, "accomplished reading" is defined as the ability to comprehend at literal and inferential levels, then assignments and assessments must mirror this view, most likely through written answers to comprehension questions and multiple-choice tests. This section briefly summarizes several of these ways of thinking about reading. While there is certainly overlap among levels and types of reading, in other ways they are quite distinct, and teachers will want to decide which best mesh with their favored teaching approaches and the needs of their students.

Reading Skills

A traditional way of viewing reading in secondary schools is as a collection of reading comprehension skills. Comprehension skills apply to both narrative and expository texts and include retelling, drawing inferences, finding or stating the main idea, summarizing, sequencing, distinguishing fact and opinion or cause and effect, recognizing organizational structures, adjusting the rate of reading to fit the difficulty of the text or purpose for reading, and evaluating the content for accuracy and consistency (Alvermann & Phelps, 1998; Readence, Bean, & Baldwin, 1995). Although workbooks for practicing these skills are available, they tend to fail to account for student motivation and background. By high school, it is generally most effective to approach such skills through short review lessons, modeling, and practicing the skill in the context of class readings.

Literal, Inferential, and Applied/Evaluative Comprehension

The work of Herber (1978), Raphael (1986), and others identifies three levels of comprehension related to the roles of the reading selection and the reader. Literal comprehension calls for a student to read and understand the details and facts presented as they appear in a narrative or expository selection. No inferences are required, no connections are made, and there is usually a single correct answer to a literal-level comprehension question. To answer literal-level comprehension questions, students need to look "on the page" (Raphael, 1986).

Inferential comprehension requires students to make connections between details and information in the text. Readers are required to make inferences so that their experiences come into play. For example, students may need to use inferential comprehension to determine the setting of a short story or a character's motives in making a particular decision. To answer interpretive comprehension questions, students need to "search and think" (Raphael, 1986), what we often call "reading between the lines."

Applied or evaluative comprehension, also known as critical comprehension, assumes that readers have passed through the other levels and therefore calls on readers to evaluate, apply, or make additional connections. Critical comprehension questions may have numerous appropriate responses, depending on readers' experiences and beliefs. To answer critical comprehension questions, students should realize they are "on their own." Students might, for example, evaluate the ethics of a character's decision or judge how truthfully parents are depicted in several works by the same author, according to criteria they establish. Students might also analyze the effectiveness of the use of the first-person narrative, or create a prequel or sequel to a story.

In reality these three levels of comprehension overlap. Students often turn inference-level questions into critical comprehension questions when they desire to find meaning and connections with their reading. Also, what for one student is a literal-level question because of a facility for decoding and a strong vocabulary becomes for a struggling reader a matter of inference. The point of having teachers be aware of these levels of comprehension isn't so they can plan and then correctly label questions for class discussion, nor should discussions begin with literal-level questions, move to inference-level questions, and conclude with applied or evaluative questions. Rather, the quest is always for critical comprehension, and we need to recognize when and where students falter.

Students who experience reading difficulties may benefit from a technique called QAR (Question-Answer-Response), which through modeling and practice allows students to learn that there are different types of questions and that these different types of questions require different sources of information to answer (Raphael, 1986). The three levels of comprehension are explained to students, they discuss sample questions for these levels, and models of answers are provided and practiced. That different questions might require different ways of thinking is new information to many high school students, a strong indication that somewhere along the line they have missed something important.

Dimensions of Reader Response

Another way of thinking about types or levels of reading emerges from reader response theory. Wilhelm (1997) has identified ten dimensions of reader response:

- entering the story world
- showing interest in the story action
- relating to characters
- visualizing (seeing) the story world
- elaborating on the story world
- connecting literature to life
- considering significance
- recognizing literary conventions
- recognizing reading as a transaction (accept, reject, or resist the author's vision)
- evaluating an author, and the self as reader (p. 157–69)

For each of these ten dimensions, Wilhelm lists student behaviors, possible questions to ask, and activities. In "recognizing reading as a transaction," for example, reader behaviors include recognizing an implied author or critiquing an author's choices. Questions that might be asked to get at this type of response include "What kind of person is the author?" and "Do you agree with how the author sees the world?" Another question for this dimension of response is "What do you feel is the most significant word, passage, or event from the story?" (p. 167). Activities that could promote this kind of response include a dramatic interview or debate with the author or creating the author's high school yearbook page (p. 168).

While Wilhelm's dimensions of response imply a variety of reading skills and comprehension levels, they clearly focus most strongly on engagement and the connections between readers and a literary work. Wilhelm contends that these responsive dimensions are key to successful reading and literary understanding, and yet they are sometimes assumed or neglected. When we draw out students' responses as part of our teaching, we encourage active and thoughtful reading.

Beginning Reading Instruction and High School Connections

Perhaps the most mysterious area of reading for many high school teachers involves early reading instruction. Traditionally, it has been assumed that high school teachers don't need to know about beginning reading because their students are well beyond that level of instruction. This simply is not always the case. The following summary of beginning reading instruction is intended to demystify the process—although not to transform English teachers into developmental or remedial reading specialists.

Sight Word Knowledge

Sight words are those that a reader can "see and say" instantly. Teaching sight words is essential in beginning reading instruction because the English language is so phonetically inconsistent and many common words simply can't be "sounded out." Attending to sight words also makes sense because perhaps "100 words account for about 50% of the words in printed materials" (Crawley & Merritt, p. 11), so that instant recognition of half the words in a selection would greatly increase reading fluency. In teaching sight words, teachers use a variety of activities including labeling objects in the classroom, labeling pictures in a book with sticky notes, or having students create personal dictionaries with magazine pictures or sketches for each sight word.

Additionally, beginning readers might create personal word banks, complete word sorts, or participate in a language experience approach (LEA) lesson in order to learn sight words. A word bank consists of words (often printed on index cards) the student can recognize at sight. Students can review the words they know by going through the cards as quickly as possible or by sorting them according to any type of category that applies: animals, food, places, words with the long vowel sounds, number of syllables, etc. Cards can also be arranged into sentences or used in games such as Concentration. In an LEA activity, a student discusses an experience or event and then dictates a story about it to the teacher or an aide. The student and teacher can then read and reread the dictated story. Because the student is the source of the story, motivation is high for the student to learn the story's words.

High school students with poor sight word vocabularies often need attention from a reading specialist who can determine the reasons for this difficulty. Instruction for students will vary according to these reasons. Many students with limited sight word vocabularies, however, benefit from time for independent reading of accessible books and other materials. They may also benefit from small-group lessons or activities that focus on attending to context and meaning. Word banks, word sorts, and LEA activities may be particularly appropriate when English is a student's second language. A number of adult basic word lists of one hundred to almost four hundred sight words are widely available (Crawley & Merritt, 2000). These include words such as *the, of, down, these, every, below, enough, often,* and *because.* For competent high school readers, pronouncing and practicing difficult, long, or phonetically irregular character names or places is a helpful practice; essentially, students are expanding their sight word vocabularies.

Decoding

Decoding means figuring out (not recognizing at sight) and pronouncing a word, either aloud or silently. Phonics, structural analysis, and context are the three components of decoding, and all three make important contributions to reading ability. Phonics instruction involves students' recognition that sounds are represented by the letters in words, what is commonly called sound-symbol correspondence. The first phases of phonics instruction help students hear different sounds (auditory discrimination or phonemic awareness) and see and recognize different

letters (visual discrimination). Different types of sound-symbol corre-
spondences are presented in Table 1.1. Typically, beginning readers
learn several consonants and several short vowels; these can be combined to create "word families," and soon students can be expected to
sound out new words. Additional consonants and long vowels are introduced and practiced, and gradually students learn consonant
blends, silent consonants, vowel digraphs, and the like.

Structural analysis refers to morphemic analysis, or how readers
recognize prefixes, suffixes, roots, and syllabic divisions to help them

Table 1.1. Components of Phonics

---

1. Consonant sounds

consonants (*s, t, r, b, d,* etc.)

consonant digraphs (a consonant digraph consists of two consonants that
together represent one sound: *sh, wh, th, ch, sk, kn, wr, ng, qu*)

consonant blends (a consonant blend consists of two or more consonants
sounded together so that each can be heard: *cl, gl, sn, sw, tr;* initial and final
positions)

substituting initial consonant sounds (as in *fat, sat, mat, cat*)

substituting final consonant sounds (as in *fat, fan, fad*)

consonant irregularities (as in the hard and soft *c* sounds in *cent* and *cough* or as
in the silent *g* in *night* or *gnat*)

contractions (*n't*)

2. Vowel sounds

short vowel sounds (*bit, fin; sat, mad*)

long vowel sounds (*meat, seen; make, main*)

the schwa sound (*much, fun*)

combination of vowel sounds in a single word (*making, reconnect*)

exceptions to vowel rules

dipthongs (a dipthong consists of two vowels blended together to form a compound speech sound: *cloud, boy, cow*).

3. Syllabication rules

prefixes and suffixes

compound words

dividing between consonants

doubling a final consonant to add a word ending

accents

decode. If a student can recognize the prefix "re" in the word *resubmit*, the word can often be broken into two recognizable units and thus decoded. High school English teachers often encourage students to use context clues to guess at the meaning of a word, but context—the words and sentence that surround an unknown word—can help with decoding as well. Phonics, structural analysis, and context can also be used in combinations. For example, a reader may use both initial consonant sound and context to determine an unknown word.

What roles do phonics and structural analysis play in high school reading? Too much attention to phonics cues is symptomatic of material that is too difficult for a reader or of a reader who is not yet fluent in English. Or it may be that the reader isn't especially interested in the text or has limited sight word recognition. Sometimes patterns of phonics difficulties can be detected, and a quick lesson may be beneficial. If several students consistently have problems decoding lengthy words, for example, and similar difficulties also arise in spelling, a review of how to break long words into manageable chunks could be helpful.

Additionally, struggling high school readers may benefit from an overall decoding strategy, such as the following:

1. Skip the word and finish the sentence. If comprehended, simply continue.

2. Use context clues.

3. Use context clues plus initial sound or recognizable pieces of the word.

4. Ask for help from the teacher, a parent, or another reader.

5. Continue reading for meaning (Warren, 1999).

Making a Difference as Teachers of Reading

I like to ask teacher candidates or teachers in my university Content Area Literacy, Methods of Teaching English, and Literature Issues classes why reading matters, what difference it makes. I am always inspired by the passion of their answers:

- Reading lets us experience lives in other times and in other places.
- Reading allows us to stretch and exercise our imaginations.
- Reading lets us learn, giving us power.
- Reading develops empathy and understanding of others.
- Reading lets us escape.

- Reading shows us how others have handled situations similar to our own, or see how others have coped with difficult circumstances.
- Reading lets us know how the world was, how it is, and how it might be.
- Reading inspires us to be better human beings and citizens.
- Reading lets us have fun and can make us laugh.

Janet Allen (1995) would add to this list that reading lets us "know we're not alone" (p. 158).

While these answers aren't exactly the stuff of standards or phonics or reading process, they are about the joy of reading, and they may best capture why we high school English teachers should consider ourselves teachers of reading. We make a difference when we plan a variety of reading approaches, supply a variety of reading materials, consider different types and levels of reading, and provide struggling readers with the support they need for success.

References

Allen, J. (1995). *It's never too late: Leading adolescents to lifelong literacy*. Portsmouth, NH: Heinemann.

Alvermann, D. E., & Phelps, S. F. (1998). *Content reading and literacy: Succeeding in today's diverse classrooms* (2nd ed.). Boston: Allyn & Bacon.

Anaya, R. (1994). *Bless me, Ultima*. New York: Warner Books.

Angelou, M. (1970). *I know why the caged bird sings*. New York: Random House.

Atwell, N. (1998). *In the middle: New understandings about writing, reading, and learning* (2nd ed.). Portsmouth, NH: Boynton/Cook.

Bracey, G. W. (1997). What happened to America's public schools? *American Heritage, 48*(7), 38–49.

Carlson, L., Ed. (1994). *Cool salsa: Bilingual poems on growing up Latino in the United States*. New York: Fawcett-Juniper.

Carr, E., & Ogle, D. (1987). K-W-L Plus: A strategy for comprehension and summarization. *Journal of Reading, 30*, 626–31.

Cisneros, S. (1983). *The house on Mango Street*. New York: Arte Publico Press.

Claggett, F. (1996). *A measure of success: From assignment to assessment in English language arts*. Portsmouth, NH: Boynton/Cook Heinemann.

Claggett, F., Reid, L., & Vinz, L. (1999). *Daybook of critical reading and writing*. Wilmington, MA: Great Source Education Group.

Crawley, S. J., & Merritt, K. (2000). *Remediating reading difficulties* (3rd ed.). Boston: McGraw-Hill.

Crew, L. (1989). *Children of the river*. New York: Delacorte Press.

Daniels, H. (1994). *Literature circles: Voice and choice in the student-centered classroom*. York, ME: Stenhouse.

Dunning, S., Lueders, E., Nye, N. S., Gilyard, K., & Worley, D. A., Eds. (1995). *Reflections on a gift of watermelon pickle . . . and other modern verse* (2nd ed.). Glenview, IL: Scott, Foresman.

Ericson, B. (1997, February). *Incorporating multicultural literature in secondary English classes: What's being used? How's it being taught?* Paper presented at the California Association of Teachers of English Conference, San Francisco, CA.

Fleischmann, P. (1988). *Joyful noise: Poems for two voices*. New York: Harper & Row.

Gallo, D. R. (Ed.) (1993). *Join in: Multiethnic short stories by outstanding writers for young adults*. New York: Delacorte Press.

Harris, P. (1999). NCTE's Reading Initiative thrives. *The Council Chronicle, 8*(4), 1, 3. Urbana, IL: National Council of Teachers of English.

Haynes, D., & Landsman, J. (Eds.). (1998). *Welcome to your life: Writings for the heart of young America* (pp. 79–83). Minneapolis, MN: Milkweed Editions.

Herber, H. (1978). *Teaching reading in content areas* (2nd ed.). Englewood Cliffs, NJ: Prentice-Hall.

Hurston, Z. N. (1991). *Their eyes were watching God*. New York: HarperCollins. (Original work published 1937)

Janeczko, P. B. (Ed.). (1983). *Poetspeak: In their work, about their work*. Scarsdale, NY: Bradbury Press.

Markandaya, K. (1990). *Nectar in a sieve*. New York: New American Library.

Martinez, V. (1996). *Parrot in the oven: Mi vida*. New York: HarperCollins.

Moyers, B. (1995). *The language of life: A festival of poets*. J. Haba (Ed.). New York: Doubleday.

Myers, M. (1996). *Changing our minds: Negotiating English and literacy*. Urbana, IL: National Council of Teachers of English.

Myers, W. D. (1988). *Fallen angels*. New York: Scholastic.

National Council of Teachers of English and International Reading Association. (1996). *Standards for the English language arts*. Newark, DE: IRA, and Urbana, IL: NCTE.

Ogle, D. (1986). K-W-L: A teaching model that develops active reading of expository text. *Reading Teacher, 39*, 563–70.

Raphael, T. (1986). Teaching question-answer relationships, revisited. *Reading Teacher, 39*, 516–22.

Readence, J. E., Bean, T. W., & Baldwin, R. S. (1995). *Content area literacy: An integrated approach* (5th ed.). Dubuque, IA: Kendall/Hunt.

Sasaki, R. W. (1991). *The loom and other stories*. St. Paul, MN: Graywolf Press.

Staples, S. F. (1989). *Shabanu: Daughter of the wind*. New York: Knopf.

Tan, A. (1989). *The Joy Luck Club*. New York: Putnam's.

Thomas, J. C. (1990). *A gathering of flowers: Stories about being young in America*. New York: HarperCollins.

Vacca, R. T., & Vacca, J. L. (1999). *Content area reading: Literacy and learning across the curriculum* (6th ed.). New York: Longman.

Warren, G. (1999). Decoding strategies. Class handout, California State University, Northridge.

Wilhelm, J. D. (1997). *"You gotta BE the book": Teaching engaged and reflective reading with adolescents*. New York: Teachers College Press and Urbana, IL: National Council of Teachers of English.

Wolff, V. E. (1993). *Make lemonade*. New York: Henry Holt.

2 Word Matters: Teaching and Learning Vocabulary in Meaningful Ways

Janet S. Allen
University of Central Florida

Words form the thread on which we string our experiences.

Aldous Huxley

It stuns me today to consider how many days and hours my students sat looking up and copying words from a dictionary during the twenty years I spent teaching high school English and reading classes. Each novel we read gave me a new list of words for students to look up, define, use in sentences, and memorize for a quiz.

"Which definition do you want?"

"The one that fits the context."

"So, can we just put the first one? The shortest one?"

"Put the one the makes sense."

"None of them make sense!"

And so it went. With each passing year, I became more aware of how ineffective this type of vocabulary instruction was, but I could not figure out what to do differently. Our school district purchased programmed vocabulary books; I used these, and students didn't know the words any better the Monday following Friday's test than they had the week before. I made lists of words I heard on television or read in the newspapers. When I tried to connect these words to the ones we had defined the week before, the students couldn't remember those words. I stopped assigning vocabulary, and students asked, "Why aren't we doing any just plain English stuff?" I had fallen into a pit all too familiar in our teaching and learning: I knew what I was doing was not working, but I didn't know what else to do.

Reading Matters

During those years when I had no idea what to do if I stopped assigning vocabulary words, I decided just to spend time reading to my students. I don't regret those days. If I had to err in any direction, I think using the time for reading was a productive move. Baker, Simmons, and Kameenui (1995) cite Anderson and Nagy's (1991) and Baumann and Kameenui's (1991) research in support of the importance of reading: "Reading is probably the most important mechanism for vocabulary growth throughout a student's school-age years and beyond" (p. 7). Sarah, a tenth-grade student in my reading class, would agree. She came to class one day after reading *The Crucible* and handed me a note telling me about a boy she liked. In language more typical of John Proctor than students in northern Maine, she said, "I think on him softly from time to time." Reading was changing the language that Sarah used to talk and write.

> *I had fallen into a pit all too familiar in our teaching and learning: I knew what I was doing was not working, but I didn't know what else to do.*

So how do we make the most of those reading moments in our English classes? How does reading actually help students get ready for the SAT? How can we be sure that students are really learning new words during reading? With all of the professional talk these days about balanced reading programs, this is one of the places where the balance has to occur. In classrooms where teachers have made diverse and rich choices for daily read-alouds and shared reading (students follow in individual texts as the teacher or another fluent reader reads the text aloud), students are exposed to an incredible variety of words. In Howe's young adult novel *The Watcher*, the narrator says to herself, "Your head is an orphanage for words" (p. 121). Reading, and the talk which bubbles around that reading, increases students' word knowledge dramatically.

An example of the talk that can precede and accompany the shared reading of a novel occurred in Kyle Gonzalez's classroom just as students were beginning their shared reading of Sparks's *It Happened to Nancy*. Students were working with a visiting science educator in order to better understand communicable diseases before continuing to read this book, which consists of journal entries from an adolescent with AIDS. From the discussion, it is obvious that Kyle allows lots of room for readers to expand their knowledge of language. The discussion begins with a student voice, with the science teacher's responses following.

"She got HIV."

"Is there a difference between HIV and AIDS?"

"No, man."

"What do I mean when I say something is contagious?"

"Something catching. You be around those germs. Germs spread."

"How else can these things get from one person to another?"

"Touching. STD's. Saliva. Toilet seats."

"Is there a difference between bacteria and a virus? Let's see if we can do something to figure some of this out. Does anyone know what a simulation is?"

"Artificial hologram. Work in simulators. Stuff that might be dangerous so we can pretend?"

The conversation continued with references to *It Happened to Nancy*, textbooks, and the experiments they were conducting. At each turn, the visiting science teacher pushed the students to make sure they understood the language they were using and adding to the words already in their repertoire.

Fortunately, these teachable moments do not occur only in English classes. As Baker, Simmons, and Kameenui (1995) explain, "One of the best ways to facilitate greater independence in vocabulary growth is through the strategic integration of vocabulary learning opportunities in multiple curricular areas" (p. 14). In math class, a teacher might use Juster's *The Phantom Tollbooth* as an opportunity to build rich context around the concept of infinity. After several pages of concrete examples, the Mathemagician in the book ends his discussion of the word by saying, "There you'll find the land of Infinity, where the tallest, the shortest, the biggest, the smallest, and the most and the least of everything are kept" (pp. 191–92).

Reading provides the opportunity to talk about interesting uses of language that may be unfamiliar to students in our classes. In one of my favorite read-alouds, a short story by Paul Jennings entitled "A Mouthful," the narrator talks about Anna "pulling a terrible face" when she sees a cat mess on her bed. In Gary Blackwood's *The Shakespeare Stealer*, the main character explains the origin of his name: "'Och, the poor little pigwidgeon!' From that unfortunate expression came the appellation of Widge, which stuck to me for years, like pitch." In reading, students receive repeated exposure to words and phrases they might never encounter in daily conversations with friends or watching television.

Shared reading also provides ample opportunity for students to not only hear the words but also to associate the words with the rich context of the surrounding text. In his book *Three Arguments against Whole Language and Why They Are Wrong* (1999), Krashen says, "Poor readers appeared to be influenced more by the overall context. In addition, poor readers appeared to profit more from helpful context" (p. 22).

In my teaching experience, I have found that if words or phrases have been critical in our shared reading of a text, students remember and use those words or phrases in writing and conversation long after I might have thought they would have forgotten them. For example, in Dennis Covington's novel of a young boy who is placed in a state institution for the handicapped solely because of his unusual appearance (his eyes are set close to the sides of his head), discussion of the word *peripheral* becomes an issue when the museum curator tries to help the boy use binoculars:

> "Try looking a little more to the side," Mr. Howell said. "Distant lights are brighter when viewed peripherally."
> "What does that mean?" I asked.
> "Sometimes things are clearer when you don't look at them head on," he answered. (*Lizard*, p. 150).

These examples highlight the three properties of vocabulary discussion that have been identified as increasing reading comprehension (Nagy, 1988): integration, repetition, and meaningful use. When readings are varied, moving from poetry to news articles, from essays and novels to lateral thinking puzzles, readers encounter a rich language they might otherwise never come in contact with. Skilled readers actually increase their word knowledge through the independent reading they do in each reading experience, but many of our students are not skilled readers. Shared reading experiences help bridge that gap as students see and hear words used in meaningful contexts; these words and concepts then become part of the knowledge and vocabulary readers take into their independent reading. But is reading all that is needed to improve reading fluency and comprehension?

Word Study

Concepts and words that are critical to the understanding of texts, to being conversant in school and life settings, and as tools for written communication often need more in-depth study than can be derived from encounters with reading. Further, students need to see demonstrations of ways in which readers come to know unknown words when they are encountered in writing or speech. For most of my teaching career, the only strategies I could give my students were those I still hear today: Look it up in the dictionary or figure it out from the context. Word study can provide students with several ways to expand their word knowledge base and develop strategies for independence.

Baker, Simmons, and Kameenui (1995) cite five principles of instructional design to increase vocabulary with diverse learners: primed background knowledge, mediated scaffolding, conspicuous strategies, strategic integration, and judicious review. Application of these instructional designs—not as ten-minute blocks of instruction added to an already packed curriculum, but as part of the way we approach teaching and learning on an ongoing basis—will help most students increase their word and their world knowledge.

Primed Background Knowledge

I once heard Frank Smith say that what was behind the eye was more important than what was in front of the eye. It is the knowledge that students already have in their heads that is so critical to their reading of most texts. Many of our students, however, do not have the language in their heads to match the content we are trying to study together. Whether reading about the Globe Theatre or the 1963 Sunday School bombing in Birmingham, students don't often bring the language of the time or event to the reading. Finding ways to build that background knowledge and give them some of the needed language through video clips, poetry, music, art, essays, news articles, interviews, or artifacts helps students then move into independent reading of texts based on other times, places, and events. I learned as much about the Globe Theatre and the climate for playwrights from Blackwood's *The Shakespeare Stealer* as I have from any text I've read. Dudley Randall's poem "The Ballad of Birmingham," when combined with the *Time* article on the Sunday School bombing that appears in *Bridges and Borders: Diversity in America* (Knauer, 1994), gives readers language, emotion, and factual knowledge to take into their reading and study. This kind of preparation can be done for all works of literature. Students not only develop a deeper understanding of the language involved, but they also usually have a more memorable response to the literature because of this brief time spent priming their background knowledge.

Mediated Scaffolding and Conspicuous Strategies

Students need to see active demonstrations of readers grappling with unknown words. Mediated scaffolding occurs when we show students ways to determine unknown words when they encounter them. Simply saying "Use the context" has almost no impact on most students. Students need to see *how* to use context. As part of our work together, students need to see us using graphs, charts, pictures, glossaries, footnotes, and parentheticals to help us understand words. They need to hear us stop to think aloud about the voice and tone used in a text as a way of inferring word meaning. They also need to see us going back to certain words or phrases after we have gained more information from the surrounding text as well as the larger text. When we come to the end of the chapter and we have some new information about a word that occurred at the beginning of the chapter, it's important to say to students, "Oh, now that I've read this, I need to go back and look at that word again." This mediation shows students how we go about making sense out of what we read and provides a model for them to do the same.

Some concepts are so important in texts we are studying or in life that we want students to understand not only the concept but also words related to the concept. In those cases, with some students we need a conspicuous way to make the concept and its related words memorable. I have found that using graphic organizers for this purpose is a useful way to help focus discussion around a concept. Most students have heard the word *prejudice,* for example, but they may have formed some broad (and perhaps faulty) understandings of the word. The word questioning organizer in Figures 2.1 and 2.2 helps further students' understanding of this concept. The target word is listed in the center, and then students look at the word parts to try to determine meaning. This structural analysis helps students learn or review prefixes and root word meanings. In this case, most students would recognize *pre* as meaning "before" and *judge* as "making an evaluation." Students then move on to guess about the meaning of the word based on the word parts. This particular class has decided that based on the word parts, *prejudice* means "making a judgment before you know something" ("facts and stuff"). They then describe characteristics of the word and actions that come from the word by listing what it is and what it is not. These students have decided that prejudice is "ignorant, unfair, narrow-minded, intolerant, and stupid" and that it is not "fair, educated, or right."

Students are then asked to brainstorm other words they predict they might encounter in an article, story, or news report that contains the word *prejudice.* This class came up with the following list of words:

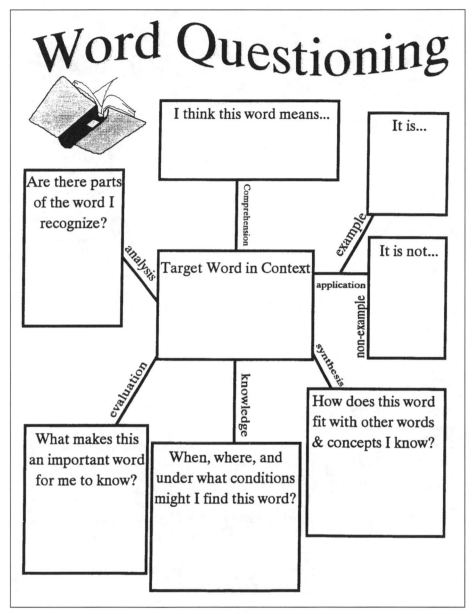

Figure 2.1. Word Questioning Graphic Organizer

hate, sexist, racist, minority, stereotype, bigot, dissin', discrimination, unfair.
This category helps students connect words to a larger concept so that
subsequent encounters with one of these words will trigger the concept
word. Words listed here might become our Word of the Day for in-depth

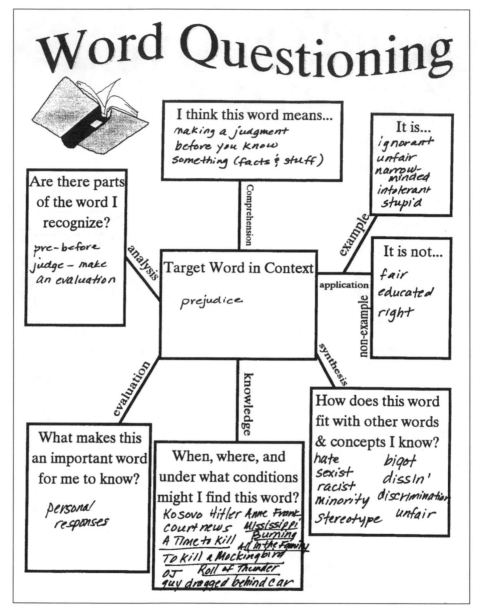

Word Questioning

I think this word means...
making a judgment
before you know
something (facts & stuff)

It is...
ignorant
unfair
narrow-
minded
intolerant
stupid

Are there parts of the word I recognize?
pre - before
judge - make
an evaluation

Comprehension

analysis

example

Target Word in Context

prejudice

application

synthesis

It is not...
fair
educated
right

non-example

evaluation

knowledge

What makes this an important word for me to know?
personal
responses

When, where, and under what conditions might I find this word?
Kosovo Hitler Anne Frank
court news Mississippi
Burning
A Time to Kill All in the Family
To Kill a Mockingbird
OJ Roll of Thunder
guy dragged behind car

How does this word fit with other words & concepts I know?
hate   bigot
sexist   dissin'
racist
minority   discrimination
stereotype unfair

Figure 2.2. Completed Word Questioning Graphic Organizer

study on another day. Then we ask students to give specific instances of where they might encounter the word *prejudice*. These students create a long list: Kosovo, court news, *A Time to Kill*, *To Kill a Mockingbird*, O. J., guy dragged behind the car, Hitler, Anne Frank, *Mississippi Burning*, *All in the Family,* and *Roll of Thunder*. Students end this whole-group discussion of the concept with a brief personal statement about why this is an important word for each of us to know, an activity that brings us to the final principles in the instructional design: strategic integration and judicious review.

Strategic Integration and Judicious Review

The graphic organizer allows students to make both personal and content connections for the concept under study. The class can discuss various uses they have heard of the word, such as "prejudicing the jury" or "prejudicial evidence." They can discuss evidence they have seen that reflects prejudice: what it looks like, sounds like, and feels like, as well as personal experiences with the word or concept. They can also review the word in relation to content knowledge: historical events, literature, current events. This concept then becomes a reference point for other related or oppositional words that are studied. Students' word banks become cumulative because the words have been studied in connection with students' life experiences as well as their language experiences.

What Really Matters

What really matters to me is that students love words, as I do. They don't need to love the same words I love; I just want them to feel the excitement I feel when I learn a word that makes it easier for me to express what matters to me. In one of my classes the other day, I used the word *pejorative* with my students. I could tell they were lost, so I stopped and said, "Again, I wouldn't want you to think that I was putting that teacher down." I saw the quick flash of connection—*pejorative:* put down—and we moved on. This week in class I noticed that in three different instances students used the word *pejorative,* always with a smile at our newly shared knowledge.

It matters to me that students leave my class with words that will stay with them for life, because these are words we have shared together. I want them to have a range of language choices so they know that instead of saying, "This sucks," they have multiple ways of objecting to what is happening in their lives. They should know language that will make people stop and listen who would not do so based on "This sucks." I want them to know that authors choose words carefully to communicate to unknown others. I want them to use words carefully because they know that words have power. I want my students to agree with Samuel Beckett that "words are all we have."

References

Anderson, R., & Nagy, W. (1991). Word meanings. In R. Barr, M. Kamil, P. Monsenthal, & P. D. Pearson (Eds.), *Handbook of reading research, Vol. 2* (pp. 690–724). New York: Longman.

Baker, S. K., Simmons, D. C., & Kameenui, E. J. (1995). *Vocabulary acquisition: Curricular and instructional implications for diverse learners* (Tech. Rep. No. 14). Eugene: National Center to Improve the Tools for Educators, University of Oregon, and Washington, DC: U.S. Dept. of Education.

Baumann, J. F., & Kameenui, E. J. (1991). Research on vocabulary instruction: Ode to Voltaire. In J. Flood, J. M. Jensen, D. Lapp, & J. R. Squire (Eds.), *Handbook of research on teaching the English language arts* (pp. 604–32). New York: Macmillan.

Blackwood, G. (1998). *The Shakespeare stealer*. New York: Scholastic.

Covington, D. (1991). *Lizard*. New York: Delacorte Press.

Howe, J. (1997). *The watcher*. New York: Atheneum.

Jennings, P. (1996). A mouthful. In P. Jennings, *Uncovered! Weird, weird stories* (pp. 37–40). New York: Viking.

Juster, N. (1961). *The phantom tollbooth*. New York: Knopf.

Knauer, K. (Ed.). (1994). *Bridges and borders: Diversity in America: Readings from* Time *magazine, 1923–1994*. New York: Warner Books.

Krashen, S. (1999). *Three arguments against whole language and why they are wrong*. Portsmouth, NH: Heinemann.

Nagy, W. E. (1988). *Teaching vocabulary to improve reading comprehension*. Urbana, IL: ERIC Clearinghouse on Reading and Communication Skills and the National Council of Teachers of English/Newark, DE: International Reading Association.

Randall, D. (1971). The ballad of Birmingham. In D. Randall (Ed.), *The Black Poets* (p. 143). New York: Bantam Books.

Sparks, Beatrice (Ed.). (1994). *It happened to Nancy*. New York: Avon Flare.

3 A Literary Transfusion: Authentic Reading-Writing Connections

John Gaughan
Lockland High School and Miami University (Ohio)

L ast fall I taught a methods class for prospective secondary English teachers at Miami University in Oxford, Ohio. As part of this course, students spent four weeks in field experiences observing and participating in English classes at nearby high schools. I asked these students to write short papers about their experiences to help them sharpen their observation skills. I include four excerpts below:

> "Okay, class, I have a worksheet for you [about 'The Cask of Amontillado']."
> I thought to myself, "This is boring. . . . If I don't want to do it, I know they must hate it.
>
> Jennifer

> When the cooperating teacher asked what Grendel from *Beowulf* represented, one student said he thought Grendel may have represented man. The cooperating teacher said he was not looking for that and he would come back to that comment later (which he never did). When no one had the answer, he told them that Grendel represents evil.
>
> Deanna

> They were given fifteen vocabulary words that they were to use in sentences correctly. . . . One of the words on one worksheet was assail. Part of the definition was the explanation that assail came from a Latin word meaning to jump on. Most

students only read this portion and produced sentences like, "To assail high is good in basketball."

Stacey

What good is MUGS (mechanics, usage, grammar, and spelling) when the kids have no desire to write, their literacy vein tapped out of all its lifeblood?

Mike

Nearly twenty years after I began teaching at the high school level and thirty years after I graduated from high school, English teachers continue to drain English of its lifeblood. Using worksheets to analyze literature that students aren't interested in to begin with, assuming definitive interpretations of literary symbols, removing vocabulary from context, and teaching language as a discreet set of skills all suck out students' enjoyment from a course that should stir their blood.

Too many high school English teachers are so worried that their students won't be prepared for college if they aren't familiar with the "important" works from the British and American canons that they often refuse to relinquish any of these classics. If they scanned the shelves of college bookstores in late August, however, they'd see that in most cases, first-year English instructors ask their students to read contemporary, multicultural texts that are not typically included on high school reading lists. Better that students be prepared to read critically, to learn to express their thoughts on readings orally and in writing, and to make meaning for themselves and with their peers.

> *Nearly twenty years after I began teaching at the high school level and thirty years after I graduated from high school, English teachers continue to drain English of its lifeblood.*

To get the blood flowing in my English classes and to promote authentic reading—that is, reading that focuses on students' active participation in making meaning, as opposed to students' reliance on their teachers' knowledge and answers—I use a thematic approach that incorporates both reading and writing of contemporary and multicultural texts. The theme I want to discuss here revolves around identity and voice.

In the 1970s, Peter Townshend and The Who asked a question that we spend our lives trying to answer: "Who are you?" Billy is trying to answer it now. Thinking about where he lives, his relationship to family and friends, his popularity in school, his social position as a U.S.

citizen, Billy struggles to understand and shape his identity. On the outside, he's six feet tall and husky, with brown eyes, closely cropped hair, and a perpetual smile. Billy plays football. He's a fifth-year senior who envisions a future in the marines. He's polite to his teachers, though he doesn't like school. He freely admits to loving his mother, whom he calls his best friend. Not everyone is his friend, though. Billy is a bigot.

English teachers have a chance to help students formulate answers to the question "Who are you?" By structuring classes so students feel free to express who they are (at least at that moment), students can begin to shape an identity. Reflecting on literature relevant to their lives and discussing topics that mirror their teenage interests, they can use the classroom as a place to try on their emerging identities. This chapter is about how I structure my class so that students will give voice to who they see themselves becoming. It is also about how this class structure can support a view of authentic, student-centered reading and writing in the high school classroom.

I begin with a series of questions:

Do you celebrate Christmas at home or with relatives?

Which college will you attend?

Why do people in England drive on the wrong side of the road?

Have any of you guys ever been asked to carry cases of pop?

Did you hear Eddie Fingers this morning on EBN?

Will you girls take your husband's name when you marry?

It's not students' answers to these questions that I want them to consider but the assumptions that underlie each question. I want my classroom to be a forum for student expression, but I want students to have some understanding of how that expression is constructed. Discussing these questions sharpens their understanding: Some students aren't Christian and don't celebrate Christmas. Many students can't afford college or have no desire to continue their education. The side of the road one drives on is arbitrary—not right or wrong, but right or left. Girls can carry cases of pop, too, though they are rarely asked to in our school. Some girls will never marry, may not even be interested in the opposite sex. Most of my students listen to rap, not rock 'n' roll.

We don't know who we are without examining some of the assumptions that underlie our lives. These questions quickly make that apparent. Various positions affect identity; gender, birth order, nationality, religion, race, school, family, class, and sexuality are just a few.

I ask students to consider metaphors that reflect identity: skater, grit, yuppie, pozer, skinhead, homeboy, jock, headbanger (Pugh, 1992,

p. 33). They write about what each metaphor means to them and with which metaphor(s) they most closely identify. Misty adds some to her list: hoe (sleeps around, wears sleazy clothes); player (goes out with more than one girl at a time); wigger (tries to act black); perpetrator (spreads rumors); and sellout (forgets where he/she comes from). This last one proves a springboard to our first piece of writing.

I want students to think about the relationship of place to identity. I read aloud the children's book *Life in the Ghetto*, showing them the pictures along the way. The author, Anika D. Thomas, was thirteen when she wrote and illustrated this story about growing up in the Hill District north of Pittsburgh. Through her story, she discusses respect, apathy, behavior, family, hope, community, and identity. When we finish reading, I ask my students to write similar pieces about their hometowns.

I was surprised the first time I asked students to complete this assignment. The depressing tone of their writing overwhelmed me. Dae Dae's is representative of many student papers:

> The West Side of Lockland would be the perfect place for a "gangsta" movie. You have your drunks, drug dealers and users, bad kids running around cursing, . . . breaking into car windows, . . . breaking into stores. You can have all of the above happening on my street alone. I live on Elm Street. This is the last street in Lockland before entering Wyoming. I live the real-life "Nightmare on Elm Street."
>
> Walking home is like entering a totally different environment. I walk down West Wyoming. The chilly afternoon air and the sunless sky make my walk home seem even longer. Near the school you have the pretty houses with porches, and flowers planted all around the yard. You have pale-faced children chasing each other, laughing and playing. The sweet smell of baking enters my nose. I walk past the walking children on my way home (the children going to West Lockland)/ . . . I see tacky-looking faces with run-over shoes and holey pants. . . .
>
> I cross Wayne Avenue, and it's like crossing the New York state line. You have the half-drunk crossing guard leading your way. You cross the street to see abandoned shops and closed-down stores. Now it's starting to look like home. . . . You see cars speeding past blasting deafening music. It's also starting to sound like home. But still I walk further down the street. Further down the drain until I empty out into my home.

Dae Dae's paper continues in this vein, vividly describing the disintegration around her, until this bit of salvation:

> At the end of Walnut is Elm Street. My house is protected from the drunks and druggies by the beautiful flowers and the wire garden fence. Like a small island lost at sea. I smell the

> sweet fragrance of the roses as I cross the street. The sun is brightly shining in my face as I walk to our back yard. I sit my book bag down and look out front. We truly live as though we are the family in a bubble. My mom tells me to always keep to myself. She says the trash belongs with the other trash, . . . as though no one in Lockland has any morals and just runs wild. . . . I guess my family are the only humans in the bunch.

Dae Dae rarely spoke in my class. She stuttered, especially when she was nervous. She traced her stuttering back to an incident in grade school when a teacher criticized something she said. School had been a struggle ever since. She always wore dresses or skirts to school, never pants. Her peers picked on her because of her clothes. I discovered that her mother was religious, that Dae Dae wasn't permitted to wear pants. Looking after younger siblings adversely affected her attendance during junior year. I wondered if she would ever make it through school. Senior year she got pregnant, but despite one more obstacle, found a way to graduate. I know she will try to protect her child as her mother tried to protect her, to fence off her own island, to retain her humanity. Dae Dae may stutter when she speaks, but her writing never stutters. She finds her voice in this piece about Lockland, makes meaning by comparing the pretty houses and pale children to the "trash" on Elm Street, flowers linking both worlds. I am still overwhelmed by the depressing details of Dae Dae's life but encouraged by her conclusion and its glimmer of hope.

Little hope, however, is reflected in Billy's "Life in Arlington Heights" paper:

> We moved into one of the shittiest apartments in Arlington Heights. When I first started to move, I thought that I was going to cry. It was an old apartment building with dead bushes around the driveway. As soon as I opened the door to go into the building, the nastiest stench struck my nostrils like Evander Holyfield hitting Mike Tyson. It smelled like old, rotten milk. I thought I was going to puke. . . .
>
> When I walked in the apartment, my mother was talking to a neighbor who I know had to weigh about four hundred pounds. Her name was Ruthie. I had never met anyone that big in person. I said Hi. My mother introduced me. Her arms were as thick as my thighs. It was sick. She sat there smoking cigarettes and drinking a diet Coke. I think she needs to do a little more than just drink diet Coke. This woman needs some liposuction or something. Later that day I saw her getting into her 1976 Dodge. I thought the shocks on the driver side weren't going to hold. I'm surprised that the driver side didn't scrape when she drove down the road. . . .

I have lived here now for seven months. I don't really like it any better but have just tolerated it a little bit more. Basically, my neighbors suck, the police are assholes. For the most part, there are nothing but dirty little kids that live around here. I hope I won't live around here very long. It might drive me insane.

Billy's piece is problematic. I'm glad he wrote it. It helps me understand where he's coming from. His parents had gotten divorced, and his mom was trying to support him and his sister. Their new apartment had only two bedrooms, so they took turns sleeping on the couch. His living conditions were less than plush. But Billy's own prejudices reveal themselves. His passages about the apartment and Ruthie are descriptive. He experiments with metaphorical writing, but the content of that metaphor is racist—that African Americans smell. The familiar "sucks" continues to populate his language and his emerging identity. No one wants to suck. But if everything around you sucks (at least as you perceive those things), it is difficult to find the flowers of hope that Dae Dae does as she reflects on her life. Billy isn't there yet.

Reading *Life in the Ghetto* stimulated students' writing about their lives. The details in Thomas's account sparked their own detailed writing, generating authentic reading-writing connections. Everyone had something to say and everyone wanted to say it right. Writing these papers helped them to reflect on where they live and to place their lives in a social context. After students wrote these pieces, I got their permission to share what they had written with other teachers at a faculty meeting. Needless to say, my eyes weren't the only ones that were opened. Recognizing students' feelings about where they live helps us understand our students. This writing was meaningful not only to the writers but to their audience as well.

In a follow-up lesson, the book *The House on Mango Street* helped students think further about the effects of place on dreams and identity. In one chapter, Sandra Cisneros's protagonist Esperanza talks about her "Monkey Garden," a haven for her and her friends when they were young, "far away from where our mothers could find us" (p. 95). My student Amanda writes about a similar place, a place she used to visit with Kate and Billy:

> I had a "Monkey Garden" while I was growing up. . . . It was hidden behind an apartment complex with a long meadow to run through before reaching the trail that led you through the woods to a place that grew pink and yellow flowers and sometimes even poison ivy. Billy and Kate fell in a patch of what they thought were leaves until they were bed-ridden for a week. . . .

> We'd bring our blankets to sit on by the creek that we imag-
> ined as a beautiful river. We would go there on an adventure be-
> cause we weren't allowed to go far from home. We would skip
> rocks or bring our bathing suits and run through the creek,
> splashing and carrying on. Our place was perfect because Kate's
> mother could yell from the patio of the apartments when it was
> about time to come home. . . .
>
> So many times we thought we had been shipwrecked on
> Gilligan's Island and had to look for some sort of shelter for sur-
> vival. We'd gather sticks taller than we were and arrange them
> like a tent, draping Mom's new bed sheets over the top. We'd
> pick up blades of grass, shoving them into a cup as if we were
> cooking them to eat for dinner. In our Monkey Garden we were
> free to do almost anything we wanted without our parents has-
> sling us. . . . Our garden is still there and I often go there to think
> or just to be alone in a quiet place. There are no more pretty
> flowers, but I can still imagine how things used to be—a place so
> pure can never get ugly.

Esperanza's garden is tainted by experience. So is Billy's. Maybe
he can't imagine how things used to be, as Amanda does, or maybe he
can but realizes, as in "The End of Innocence" (Henley), that he can't go
back. The stench of his new apartment, the dead bushes out front, the
neighbors who "suck" all pervade his present, erase his past, and color
his future. Amanda's hopeful conclusion—that a place so pure can never
get ugly—doesn't work for Billy—the same Billy who used to skip rocks
and carry on until Kate's mom yelled it was time to go home. Maybe the
poison ivy still itches. Simply reading about others' experiences and
writing about where he has grown up won't eliminate the itching, but
these activities can act as a salve to soothe it so that he can move on.

We also read and write about family because, more than place,
family leaves an indelible mark on who we become. Ernest J. Gaines's
"The Sky Is Gray" helps Nicole understand why her mother treats her
differently than her younger siblings:

> It made me realize everything the mother did was to prepare
> her children for the worst. I mean she didn't know if segregation
> would ever end, so she had to teach her kids to protect them-
> selves from harm. Now if you apply that to my family, my
> mother in particular, you'll see that she does the same thing. . . .
> Since I'm the oldest, I'm supposed to protect them [her siblings]
> to keep them in line.

Tim relates to this story too because, like James in "The Sky Is Gray," he
is the "man around the house."

Two other works about family spark memories and student writing: "The Kid's Guide to Divorce" by Lorrie Moore and "Diary of a

Single Mother" by Cynthia Heimel. Moore's story is written in second person, the "kid" telling other kids how to make the best of living between two parents. I ask students to write similar pieces about family using the story as a model. Charity titled her piece "A Teenager's Guide to a Stable Family":

> Your mom will ask, "What did you do this weekend?", and you are able to tell her, even if you got trashed to the point where you couldn't walk and you told your best friend to pray for you. . . . And you can go to your mom or dad and tell them about the guy that tried, but never accomplished, taking advantage of you and they'll hold you and comfort you and they'll say, "Shhh, everything will be all right," and you'll have faith in them that it will. . . .
>
> You can go to your dad and ask for your mom and he'll say she's working, but can I help? You'll look at him funny and you'll say, "Dad, I need a woman. I'm having womanly problems." Your dad will return your odd look and say, "Well, for now, I am the woman." You'll laugh at this comment that was meant to be a joke and you'll tell him that you really need a box of tampons and he'll gladly offer to get them for you. You're a bit shocked and embarrassed for him, but only for the moment and you let him do what he has offered.
>
> Finally, after a long, hard and tiring day, you can come home to a nice warm house where dinner is always on the table and someone is always there awaiting your arrival. At dinner your parents will ask, "How was your day?", and you'll just sit there with a frown on your face. They'll sadly look at you and ask what happened. You will then break out of your silence and scream, "My whole day sucked and so does my life!" Your mom will shyly laugh and say, "Well, you're sure as hell a lot luckier than most teenagers!" You will then fall back into reality and remember just how lucky you really are.

Charity has written a number of pieces about her family since I've known her. She's acknowledged family problems with alcohol and drug abuse, but in the end her family's stability remains solid. While Moore's story is tinged with cynicism, Charity's rings sincere. By writing about her family, Charity realizes that her life does not "suck."

Cynthia Heimel's "Diary of a Single Mother" is about her struggle to raise her son alone. Each entry begins with a year, starting with 1970. Sarah uses this story as a springboard for her own piece called "Diary of an Abandoned Daughter." Her story begins in 1979: "On November 16th I was born. My mother is there but my father isn't. I should bring happiness, but I don't." Sarah relates only the events that strike her as significant in shaping her life, just as Heimel does. Sarah recalls that in 1984 her grandfather brought her doughnuts every morning before school. In 1985 he dies. Her father abandons her and her brother in 1987, but her mother gets a new boyfriend. "1988: We move in with my mother's boyfriend. He's an alcoholic drug abuser. He beats my mother. My parents' divorce is final. My father becomes an alcoholic. But I never see him."

Her mother's boyfriend becomes so abusive that Sarah and her family move in with her grandmother. Her father still isn't a part of her life, won't even accept pictures of her or her brother. Her mother remarries, but she and her new husband "fight a lot. There's never any peace." Another divorce, a new boyfriend, more moving, depression triggering thoughts of suicide, her father calling her brother more often now, "but [he] doesn't seem to remember me." Finally, the present:

> I'm sixteen now. I have a job, a car, and my license, which I established for myself. I have a new best friend. . . . I even call her mom "Mom." It's been over two years since I've told my real mom I love her. It's weird how you can love someone but not like them. I'm pretty much independent now. I have to be. I have a new boyfriend. He isn't at all like the other guys I've known. I quit relying on others to bring me happiness. I can do that for myself. I hope to go to college when I graduate. But my guess is my father won't be around to help.

Sarah's "diary" ends here. She recently graduated with a solid B average, the same boyfriend, and a baby of her own on the way. I wonder if this baby's father will be there for his child, or be the subject of another "diary" sixteen years from now. I have known countless young mothers since I began teaching at Lockland. Many, like Sarah, dream of their futures, aspire to a college education, claim their independence, quit relying on others for their happiness. Most of them have to; few of these young women ever marry their babies' fathers. Occasionally, they find ways to support their children as well as gain a college education. I hope Sarah is one of them.

The innocence of "monkey gardens," of bygone days, fades too quickly for some of our students. The reality of money problems, of absent fathers, of unexpected pregnancies, crush that innocence as only experience can. William Stafford's poem "Fifteen" reminds us of that innocence lost. As the fifteen-year-old narrator marvels at the motorcycle he finds behind the willows, its engine running, he is quickly shaken from his reverie when he finds the rider, who has flipped over the rail. "He had blood on his hand, was pale / . . . I stood there, fifteen."

Students can also write poems reflecting on a particular age or on the state of innocence that Stafford captures so well. Here is Amy's:

Innocence

A cool breeze touches my fingertips
as does the clover butterfly,
beyond my grasp, then beyond my eyes.

A small smile shines from a face high above
as its smooth polished hand caresses my crown.

Wandering through the fields of youth,
I glance toward the sky in search of genies,
in search of magic.
Tell me more of the sleeping beauties,
of the princes that slay their dragons.

As the years sweep by,
the winds of change bring forth the darkened clouds
to cover my sun,
to cover its love.

Again and again its patches of light shine upon me,
shine upon the world,
only to be smothered by the hands of destruction.

Whatever happened to the finger paints and baby dolls
of my days gone by?
Of my training wheels and Sesame Streets?

Take me back,
retrace my steps.
Follow me to my innocence.

A tear rolls down my cheek.
Remembering
what once was so simple.

Teachers, like parents, cannot protect children from experience. We have to believe, though, that having them write about their experiences, reflecting on the innocence lost, is useful to them: that their writing is therapeutic, that it may empower them, that it can extinguish the silence that sometimes paralyzes them.

I wish I could guarantee that reading and writing about these experiences will break the cycles of abandonment and abuse. But I can't. I don't know what will become of Sarah; I can only hope that when her baby is born, it will bring Sarah the happiness that Sarah didn't bring her own mother, that this baby will not have to lose its innocence so early in life, that someday this baby can remember "what once was so simple."

Though these pieces about family liberate many of my students' voices, some students are still uncomfortable opening up on paper.

Other reading-writing connections work better for them. Sometimes these student writers need to try on other identities to discover their own. When students read Salinger's *The Catcher in the Rye,* they express their feelings about Holden, interpret his dream, analyze his attachment to mummies, and react to his desire to preserve Phoebe's innocence. But they also try on his voice. Instead of addressing the content of the book, however, I ask them to imagine Holden living today and to reflect on contemporary topics. Here is an excerpt from Mike's reflection:

> People are so phony anymore. . . . Always doing things just to look good among their peers. Take, for instance, those god-dam morons that run our country. If they're not phony, who is?
>
> That bastard Bush never done a thing for this country, expect maybe Desert Storm. I admire him for his decisions during the war, but other than that, man, what a moron. I sort of feel sorry for him. I'm not sure why. I guess because he's old and all, and he did receive a pretty bad rap from the media. He sort of deserved it, though. If he would have just got up off his lazy ass and done something about the economy, maybe he could have stayed phony for another four years.
>
> Now we've got this bastard Clinton in office. If he's not a bastard lacking morals, then I don't know who is. Think about it—gays in the military, gay rights. Who's he kidding? I'm practically an atheist and even I've read the Bible.
>
> The Bible . . . there's a damn good book. A little long but good. I may never have cared for the disciples and all, but that old Jesus sure was a character.
>
> Jesus, now there's a man with some morals. Had one of the roughest lives I've ever heard of, but not once did he sin. Old Jesus . . . I felt sorry and all for him, though, because no one ever believed him. He always seemed to have some type of problem. I've talked to Jesus, once or twice you know, just in case he is listening and all. I don't think you could call me faithful, at least not Noah faithful.
>
> Noah, now that was one faithful sonuvabitch. I mean to build this big goddam ark and all when it has never even rained before. . . .

When I had asked Mike to write analytical pieces prior to this, he did just fine. His mind was more mathematical than most, so analytical writing came easy for him. Personal narrative was more difficult. This assignment freed him to express some of his own feelings, but through another's voice. I'm reminded of Kurt Vonnegut's short story "Who Am I This Time?" The protagonist Harry is shy, reserved, quiet in public, and nervous around other people, especially the opposite sex. When he takes the stage, though, he is dynamic, forceful, present. Paradoxically, asking our students to wear masks from their reading when they write can help them establish their own voices. The opinions expressed in Mike's writing about politics and morals, homosexuality and religion, are not Holden's but Mike's. In the end of Vonnegut's story, Harry finds romance, and in the end Mike will find his voice.

Reading about place, family, innocence, and experience engages students in ways that chronological surveys of British and American literature do not. Immersing students in the theme of emerging identities is something to which they can relate. The writing that follows each reading seems easy and natural to them.

The final story I want to discuss revolves around peer relationships and the pressure to conform. In Tom Perrotta's "Forgiveness," the narrator faces the biggest ethical dilemma of his life when his football coach asks the team whether Randy Dudley, one of their best players, should be forgiven so that he can play in the state championship football game. Randy had blackened his girlfriend's eye, gotten drunk later the same night, and wrecked his car after his girlfriend's father wouldn't let him speak to her. Though the team policy was clear—drinking, smoking, and drug use were prohibited during the season, "get caught and you were gone"—the coach made a locker-room speech about Christ and forgiveness just before the game was to be played. Though the narrator agrees with his best friend Rocky that Randy should not be forgiven, he wants the jacket that complements a state championship. So, along with the rest of his teammates except Rocky (who declines to play in the final game), he votes to "forgive" Randy, and his team wins the game by a touchdown.

My student teacher at the time, Tom Gaffigan, asked us to respond in writing to the following question:

> Imagine yourself in the locker room at the end of the story when Coach Whalen asked the team to vote on whether Randy should be forgiven for violating team rules. If you were the narrator, how would you vote, especially in light of your best friend's decision to vote against forgiving Randy? Be sure to explain why.

Tom asked us to exchange papers when we finished and to respond to as many of our peers' writings as possible in fifteen minutes. Following are my initial response and the three responses I received from Rachle, Billy, and Tom:

> If I had been in the narrator's shoes and only a sophomore in high school, I probably would've gone along with the team. However, I don't think I'd have been right. Rocky had guts. He knew "bullshit" when he smelled it and Coach Whalen's speech was

bullshit. He liked using Vietnam and religion to get what he wanted, but I don't think he was really patriotic or religious. Sure, I believe in forgiveness, in being "Christ-like," but Randy Dudley beat his girlfriend; he needs to suffer the consequences. I would've voted to "forgive" Randy, but I would have been wrong.

J. G.

I absolutely agree. The pressure of the team and wanting to win would have made me vote to forgive, even though it's not right.

Rachle

I disagree. I wouldn't let a team or anyone influence me in what I thought. I believe in what's the better moral thing to do. The kid was arrested. I don't know about you, but I wouldn't want to play with a criminal. Let's think about this. Football players are supposed to be "team leaders." Good players or not, "You play, you pay."

Billy

It's easy in retrospect to say I would have sided with Rocky. But, that would be as much BS as Whalen was shoveling. I agree with Mr. G. because the pressure of the moment would have made me cave in. I blame the adults in charge for not having the guts to exhibit the leadership for which they are paid. This should not have been in the players' hands.

Tom Gaffigan

When we finished, Tom asked us to pass back the papers to the person who had begun the response and to read our peers' comments. "Did anyone see a response that disagreed with what you'd written?" he asked. Nearly everyone's hand went up. Kristy said, "I think the narrator should've stuck by Rocky, but someone in here told me to 'lighten up,' that no one should hold 'grudges.' Well, I think they're wrong, that Randy deserved to be punished."

Julie said the dilemma in the locker room was never about "forgiveness," and shouldn't have been called a "vote." "This was just a way to get a star player back on the team for the championship game."

Charity identified with the "scrubs" in the story who had been kicked off the team for drinking earlier in the season but were never extended the same chance at forgiveness as Randy; they weren't good enough players. Charity works her "butt off" for sports, attends every practice, only to see more talented athletes skip practice and still "earn" starting positions. She recognizes how policies are bent for a privileged few.

Justin said, "They won without Rocky; they could've won without Randy."

Rebecca claimed Coach Whalen needed a "reality check: high school students are going to drink."

Through our oral and written responses, each of us establishes our identity. As an insecure high school student, I probably wouldn't have said a word had such a discussion taken place in my own high school English class (it never did because we never read stories like "Forgiveness"). Had I been pushed to respond, I would have said the "right thing" because I was a teacher pleaser (probably a function of the oldest-child syndrome). As a teacher far removed from adolescence, I could admit in my present response what I wouldn't have admitted then.

Rachle is a teacher pleaser, too (also an oldest child). Billy says he would do the "better moral thing," that he would not be influenced by his teammates, but earlier in the semester when we had watched *Casualties of War* (DePalma, 1990), a film set in Vietnam, he said in discussion that he would have followed orders to rape a young girl in order to be part of his platoon. Charity finds a personal connection. No one wants to admit being a "scrub," but Charity is more secure than most of her peers. She puts her athletic talent into perspective. She may be number two in her class academically, but athletically she's a scrub.

Creating opportunities for students to read and write about their lives—to reflect on their neighborhoods, their families, and the innocence of the past—through literature and poetry; to try on different voices, such as mimicking Holden Caulfield; to think and write about ethical dilemmas, is essential for students to be able to forge their own identities. Self-expression is what makes us human. Reflecting on that expression helps us understand our humanity.

When students' literary diets consist solely of classical literature, their models for writing are dated. When all of the authors they are exposed to have western European roots, they may never see themselves mirrored in the texts they read. When teachers shift their focus to thematic units, students may not learn about literary traditions such as Romanticism and Realism, but the reading and writing they do will be authentic and engage their evolving selves.

Each of those selves is shaped by the societal forces that pervade individual lives: neighborhood and school, family and peers. Reflecting on these forces can help students understand the people they have become and help shape the people they are becoming. Dae Dae sees flowers amidst the "trash"; Amanda finds beauty in her "monkey garden"; Sarah learns self-reliance.

Separating language, vocabulary, reading, and writing from meaningful contexts drains the lifeblood from the English curriculum.

Studying language in the context of students' lives can stir their blood and ignite their passions. Reading and writing in the context I have described might sometimes make us blush, but it will never bore us. Let's put some color back into the curriculum by rethinking what we teach and how we teach it. Let's stir the literary blood.

References

Cisneros, S. (1989). *The house on Mango Street*. New York: Vintage.

Depalma, B. (Director). (1990). *Casualties of war* [Film]. RCA/Columbia Pictures Home Video.

Gaines, E. J. (1997). The sky is gray. In E. J. Gaines, *Bloodline* (pp. 83–117). New York: Vintage Contemporaries.

Heimel, C. (1993). Diary of a single mother. In J. Sommers & C. Lewiecki-Wilson (Eds.), *From community to college: Reading and writing across diverse contexts* (pp. 46–51). New York: St. Martin's Press.

Henley, D. (1989). The end of the innocence. On *The end of the innocence* [CD]. Los Angeles: Geffen.

Moore, L. (1986). The kid's guide to divorce. In B. Weber (Ed.), *Look who's talking: An anthology of voices in the modern American short story* (pp. 143–51). New York: Washington Square Press.

Perrotta, T. (1994). Forgiveness. In T. Perrotta, *Bad haircut: Stories of the seventies* (pp. 92–113). New York: Berkley Books.

Pugh, S. L. (1992). *Bridging: A teacher's guide to metaphorical thinking*. Urbana, IL: National Council of Teachers of English and Bloomington, IN: ERIC Clearinghouse on Reading and Communication Skills.

Salinger, J. D. (1972). *The catcher in the rye*. Boston: Bantam Books.

Stafford, W. (1970). Fifteen. In R. Peck (Ed.), *Sounds and silences: Poetry for Now* (p. 33). New York: Dell.

Thomas, A. D. (1991). *Life in the ghetto*. Kansas City, MO: Landmark Editions.

Townsend, P. (1983). Who are you? On *Who's Greatest Hits* [CD]. Universal City, CA: MCA Records.

Vonnegut, K. (1972). Who am I this time? In K. Vonnegut, *Welcome to the Monkey House* (pp. 14–27). New York: Dell.

4 An After-School Reading Intervention Program for Struggling Readers

Linda L. Flammer
Francis Polytechnic High School, Los Angeles

Juan is fifteen, a conscientious ninth grader who attends school regularly and earns mostly Cs and a few Bs. Polite, punctual, and cooperative, he is a pleasure to have in my English class. He's the kind of student who seems to want to do well, but who doesn't stand out as either exceptional or problematic. Yet there is one looming problem for this young person: he is reading at about the third-grade level.

What do we English teachers, who haven't been trained as reading teachers, do for Juan and the many others like him who sit in urban high school English classes reading six, seven, or eight years behind grade level? Where do we begin? How do we get through core literature with classrooms full of kids for whom the core literature is virtually unreadable?

My high school of 3,700 students is located in the eastern San Fernando Valley of the greater Los Angeles area. Ninety percent of Polytechnic's students are of Latino background, over 75 percent qualify for federal lunch programs, and approximately one-third are designated limited English proficient. Reading scores on the Stanford 9 test recently fell in the 17th, 16th, and 21st percentiles for ninth, tenth, and eleventh grades, respectively.

Concerned with these low test scores and uncertain how to provide students like Juan with the help they need, a team of teachers at my school wrote and received a grant to support The Literacy Center, TLC@Poly, an intervention program aimed at improving literacy for ninth-grade students reading at or below the fifth-grade level. What follows in this chapter is a description of The Literacy Center program, beginning with an overview of the literacy coaches.

The Literacy Coaches

Members of The Literacy Center teaching cadre, in addition to their regular teaching duties, serve as literacy coaches for the students in the program. While the English, ESL, and special education teachers who serve as coaches bring specialized expertise that is beneficial to others in the group, they also receive training in research-based literacy strategies for secondary students. They attended a one-week summer institute ("It's Never Too Late Literacy Institute") conducted by Dr. Janet Allen, and they participate in monthly day-long workshops to practice various decoding, comprehension, vocabulary, and assessment strategies and to preview young adult literature and other "high interest" materials.

Much of the early professional development of the literacy coaches involved rethinking conceptions of reading and reading improvement strategies. One key breakthrough came in renewing our view of reading as an active, meaning-making process, rather than the passive activity practiced by so many of our students. This meant renewing our belief in the value of prereading activities intended to tap student beliefs and experiences. High schoolers bring with them to the classroom and to the reading experience a wealth of information garnered from life experiences—although, admittedly, not always the kinds of life experiences we would wish for them! Making connections between life experiences and reading has become a key component of TLC activities.

What do we English teachers, who haven't been trained as reading teachers, do for Juan and the many others like him who sit in urban high school English classes reading six, seven, or eight years behind grade level?

Another crucial issue for literacy coaches involves making distinctions among kinds of readings and knowing when to use different kinds of reading. Allen uses the term "read-aloud" to describe a situation in which reading is done by an expert, practiced reader and listeners hear the reading without looking at the text (Allen & Gonzalez, 1998). This can create interest in a topic, spark curiosity, and get kids thinking, laughing, and feeling. Reading aloud is an effective way to begin or end a class, and it involves no risk for students. Another kind of reading is "shared reading," where an expert reader reads aloud while listeners look at the text being read. Many high school teachers may feel more than a twinge of guilt when they "do the reading for" their students. It feels like something other than teaching. But teacher-researcher Allen articulates a crucial point in *It's Never Too Late:* "shared reading, . . . defined by New Zealand educators as 'eyes past print with voice support,' offers all students access to the books in [the] classroom" (1995, p. 31). Such reading allows second-language speakers to hear fluent reading in English. Shared reading also creates a no-risk atmosphere in the classroom, with the teacher modeling effective reading.

Another kind of reading is "reciprocal reading," in which the teacher and students take turns reading aloud. This is perhaps the closest to how reading is traditionally done in classrooms, but it moves away from the row-by-row droning of struggling readers. Other teachers might call this "popcorn reading," with the distinction that in reciprocal reading the teacher also participates in the oral reading process. Reciprocal reading is usually used with texts that are accessible to the majority of the students, so that a successful oral reading experience results. Finally, there is "independent" reading, which asks students to read material silently or orally on their own. Literature or other texts that are completely accessible to students should be selected so that the ease of reading reinforces a positive experience with text. Understanding and practicing different kinds of reading empowers our struggling readers.

A final element of The Literacy Center program's philosophy emerges from the work of Cambourne (1988), who studied how young children acquire language, as well as how older children learn difficult but engaging tasks outside the classroom, such as playing soccer. One finding in his work taken to heart by the literacy coaches is the value of allowing time for practice without penalty in a risk-free environment. All of these notions—reading as an active process, recognizing and practicing different kinds of reading, and allowing opportunities for risk-free practice—are central to The Literacy Center program.

The Students

Candidates for the program are students recommended by their teachers and whose reading test scores are below the fifth-grade level; most score in the range of grades 3 through 5. To be eligible for the program, students must have good attendance, work habits, and cooperation, as well as the support of their parents. Students who opt to participate agree to accept a "scholarship" to attend four ninety-minute after-

school sessions each week for five weeks. One five-week cycle was offered in each of the year-round school's three tracks during 1998–99. In
the end, ten to fifteen students participated in each cycle, so that the
program reached about forty students in the first year. For the
1999–2000 school year, Saturday morning sessions have been scheduled in an attempt to draw more qualified students to the program.

All students in the program are given the Flynt-Cooter Individualized Reading Inventory (1995), an individually administered "test"
which provides preliminary information about students' reading abilities. This individualized reading inventory (IRI) begins by having a
student give verbal descriptions of pictures, a task that can provide important clues about the language facility of second-language learners.
A student then silently reads a short passage and retells what it was
about. Next, he or she rereads the passage aloud. Passages of increasing difficulty are read silently and then orally to identify a student's independent and instructional reading levels, as well as particular
strategies the student may use in decoding. Throughout the IRI, the
test administrator keeps a running record of the student's oral language, oral reading, and comprehension skills.

Most students who participate in the program fall into one of two
categories: those who seem to have fluent oral decoding skills but lack
higher-level inferential skills, and those who appear less fluent with
oral reading, stumbling over some of the more difficult or unfamiliar
vocabulary, but who show strong literal and higher-level comprehension. This latter group seems able to use context to infer meaning for
important vocabulary, which leads them to greater comprehension.

The Literacy Center Program

The Literacy Center program is divided into two main components:
coach-led instruction during Monday and Wednesday sessions, and
learning centers during Tuesday and Thursday sessions. As a culminating activity, students create portfolios and present them in a student-led
conference evening.

Monday-Wednesday Sessions

The Monday-Wednesday sessions begin with shared reading by the
coaches from a common book. *Hatchet* (Paulsen, 1987) is a commonly
used book, selected because of its appeal for students. In *Hatchet*, Brian
Robeson is stranded in the Canadian wilderness following a small
plane crash. He must learn to survive, not only the challenges of the

wilderness, but also those of life, including his parents' divorce and his secret knowledge of what led to the divorce. Over the five weeks, students participate in a variety of activities to accompany the shared reading. For example, one day they might chart the food they love and hate, thus making connections with some of Brian's eating experiences. They make predictions, discuss their responses to anticipation-reaction guides, and complete imitative writing assignments. Students also spend time in discussion, and the coaches model questions and responses and help students analyze their own. Students react positively to these activities and discussions, all of which aim to promote students' involvement with characters, situations, and themes. This part of the Monday-Wednesday session typically runs about an hour.

Next, the coach presents a minilesson on an aspect of decoding or spelling. Students might review the "silent/magic *e*" rule, for example, and complete an accompanying activity or activities that are game-like and short. A number of coaches had good success with several variations of word walls (Cunningham, Moore, Cunningham, & Moore, 1989; Cunningham, 1994). To create a word wall, students provide examples of words from their reading or knowledge that meet a particular criterion, and these are listed on a single sheet of butcher paper that is posted in the room. Students might provide examples of words with a long *e* sound but with spellings that are different (*meat, feed, meter,* etc.), or they might think of words with the prefix "pre-". Some teachers prefer using index cards that can be displayed or stored in file folders so that all the words can later be used for different sorting activities.

These minilessons are always connected back to the reading. For example, students in a group might be asked to find examples of words with a silent *e* on different pages of *Hatchet,* a sort of scavenger hunt. Students are very receptive to these minilessons, sometimes commenting, "Oh, yeah, I think I remember something about this." When they were younger, many of these students were just learning English and unable to focus on these sorts of rules; instead, they were learning lessons such as the importance of word endings in the English language (in Spanish, word endings are less significant). Students do not view these minilessons as repetitious, but as opportunities to learn something missed at an earlier phase of education. This minilesson segment typically takes about twenty minutes.

Monday-Wednesday sessions conclude with the literacy coach reading aloud from a book or selection of his or her choice. From the poems of Shel Silverstein to the opening chapter of Gary Soto's *Buried*

Onions (1997), these readings demonstrate a teacher's obvious enjoyment of reading, provide a positive closure to the session, and introduce students to possible independent reading choices.

Tuesday-Thursday Sessions

Students in each group circulate to three learning centers during the Tuesday-Thursday sessions, spending thirty minutes at each center. In the Independent Reading Center, students make a selection from the numerous picture books, children's books, young adult books, and magazines that are available; they independently read and then respond to one of several open-ended questions in their reading logs. In the Art Center, students respond to *Hatchet,* another group book, or an independent reading book by creating a variety of art projects. They might construct a collage, write and illustrate an "I Am" poem, or produce a poster of a character or scene. Students and coaches alike see great value in this center because it encourages students to visualize the people and events in a book, an important strategy of good readers (Wilhelm, 1997). The Vocabulary Enrichment Center focuses on vocabulary development, a key aspect of reading comprehension (Readence, Bean, & Baldwin, 1998; McQuillan et al., Chapter 6 of this volume). The time at this center often begins with group reciprocal reading of the first several paragraphs of an article they choose from *USA Today* or a newsmagazine such as *Teen People.* Students identify three to five vocabulary words in the article and attempt to unlock their meanings from context or morphological clues (prefixes, suffixes, roots, syllables). The group discusses possible meanings and explains how and why they came to these definitions based on the clues. After checking a dictionary and again using the available clues, students create a poster for each word, providing the original sentence, a definition, and an illustration. This type of activity might also be completed using one or two pages from *Hatchet* or a selection from a middle school–level *Daybook of Critical Reading and Writing* (Claggett, Reid, & Vinz, 1999). Other activities in this center include creating word maps, graphic representations of synonyms, examples, and contexts for a word, and playing games such as Scrabble or Boggle.

The Culminating Activity

Each five-week TLC program culminates with student-led conferences in conjunction with student-created portfolios. For this concluding activity, students choose three pieces of work that demonstrate what they gained during The Literacy Center program, and they present ideas about how they will take what they learned back to their regular classrooms. These presentations are made to a group of peers and adults including parents, selected teachers, and administrators.

The self-assessment and reflection of the culminating activity are key ingredients throughout the program, but they are particularly evident and revealing at this point. From the conferences for 1998–99, several conclusions can be drawn about student perceptions regarding the program. Most students mentioned the Art Center as a favorite, and many students explained that they hadn't known before that "you should get a picture in your head" during reading. Other students noted the importance of making predictions and of learning that you can guess at a word or even skip over it during your reading. As one young man noted, "You don't have to just quit if you don't know the word." Others enjoyed reading the children's and young adult books on their own, sometimes confessing a first experience with reading a book in its entirety. Additionally, about 25 percent mentioned being helped by the "magic *e*" rule. Students could also describe what they needed to do when confronted with a difficult piece of reading, something they had been unable to do at the beginning of the program.

Insights and Outcomes

Interviews with the students' other teachers also point to many successes. These teachers noted an increase in participating students' willingness to read aloud and at home as part of regular class assignments. Teachers also reported that grades on projects which involved reading showed increases of at least a full letter grade. Attendance and a willingness to participate in class activities improved, not only in English classes but also in social studies, science, and math classes. While this evidence is anecdotal, coaches seem to have achieved success through working with these students in small teams; bonding with them; giving them a fun, safe, relaxed environment in which to improve; and, most important, aligning the reading experiences with the students' needs as emerging readers.

Coaches too were changed by their participation in the 1998–99 program. All the coaches took strategies learned in their training back to their regular classrooms, making strong literacy practices available to a larger number of students. Coaches also served as informal mentors or advisors to other teachers who were curious about the program and interested in learning new literacy strategies, again spreading this information more widely throughout the school. Finally, coaches described an increased awareness of the difficulty of the literature or texts they were assigning in their regular classes—and the negative impact those selections had on students when too little support for reading was provided.

The Literacy Center program and most other intervention programs offer instruction and activities beyond those found in the regular curriculum and also extend the hours of the regular school day because the needs of these students by the time they get to high school are greater than teachers can meet during regular class time. The institutional response to these seemingly overwhelming needs should not be to simply surrender and do nothing but to seek out Title I and other funding to support intervention programs. Our experiences with TLC@Poly point to the importance of creating an environment in which individual attention can be given and emotional safety assured. Training for teachers and the involvement of parents are other essential ingredients, as are a wide choice of materials appropriate to the interest and reading levels of struggling students and the time to read them. As high school English teachers, we are sometimes overwhelmed by what our struggling readers seem unable to accomplish. We must take heart in knowing that there are ways to address the literacy needs of many of these students.

References

Allen, J. (1995). *It's never too late: Leading adolescents to lifelong literacy.* Portsmouth, NH: Heinemann.

Allen, J., & Gonzalez, K. (1998). *There's room for me here: Literacy workshop in the middle school.* York, ME: Stenhouse.

Cambourne, B. (1988). *The whole story: Natural learning and the acquisition of literacy in the classroom.* Auckland, New Zealand: Ashton Scholastic.

Claggett, F., Reid, L., & Vinz, R. (Eds.). (1999). *Daybook of critical reading and writing.* Wilmington, MA: Great Source Education Group.

Cunningham, P. (1994). *Making big words: Multilevel, hands-on spelling and phonics activities.* Carthage, IL: Good Apple.

Cunningham, P. M., Moore, S. A., Cunningham, J. W., & Moore, D.W. (1989). *Reading in elementary classrooms: Strategies and observations.* New York: Longman.

Flynt, E. S., & Cooter, R. B. (1995). *Flynt-Cooter reading inventory for the classroom* (2nd ed.). Scottsdale, AZ: Gorsuch Scarisbrick.

Paulsen, G. (1987). *Hatchet.* New York: Aladdin.

Readence, J. E., Bean, T. W., & Baldwin, R. S. (1998). *Content area literacy: An integrated approach* (6th ed.). Dubuque, IA: Kendall/Hunt.

Soto, G. (1997). *Buried onions.* San Diego, CA: Harcourt Brace.

Wilhelm, J. D. (1997). *"You gotta BE the book": Teaching engaged and reflective reading with adolescents.* New York: Teachers College Press and Urbana, IL: National Council of Teachers of English.

5 A Twelfth-Grade Reading Class for Struggling Readers

Susan Schauwecker
McLane High School, Fresno, California

The twelfth graders I teach the last two class periods of the day are students who read at third- and fourth-grade levels, and their presence in these classes is based on the fact that they have taken and failed the twelfth-grade basic skills test, which serves as our district's high school exit exam, twice a year since the eighth grade. Not only do their test scores appear to demonstrate a lack of basic reading and writing skills, but they have also turned off to all reading because they have not experienced success no matter how hard they have worked. These students bring rich personal stories, but when placed in an academic setting, when competing with other students of their own age group, they simply turn off and shut down. As Janet Allen says in *It's Never Too Late*, "these students exclude themselves from participation in and enjoyment of school activities which seem to require 'good reading'" (1995, p. ix).

My senior students have little interaction with articulate, accomplished English-language speakers (and readers), in part because it isn't "cool," and in part because they lack the necessary confidence. For many, this lack of confidence is related to their language backgrounds. Speaking one or two of twenty-five different primary languages including Hmong, Tagalog, Hindi, Lao, Cambodian, Spanish, and Chinese, they function well in their own families and isolated communities, but the English-speaking world tends to intimidate them. Another factor that affects the schooling of these students is that the men are often pushed and prodded to succeed, while the women are often married mothers by the time they are fourteen years old. Therefore, the majority of my female students are women raising small children and running their own households, breaking with social custom to attend my class.

The students in these senior English classes are not exclusively from linguistically diverse backgrounds, however; nearly one-third are U.S. citizens whose families cannot be classified as recent immigrants.

Their literacy challenges appear to stem from social, socioeconomic, or developmental causes. Another cause is likely educational: these students have not had direct reading instruction since the third grade. If they did not function as readers by the third grade, they simply haven't functioned academically at school since then. These social, socioeconomic, developmental, and educational circumstances combine to create an appalling dropout rate at my high school. Approximately 1,500 ninth graders arrive every school year, and four years later those students who graduate number between 350 and 400. That's over a thousand students who have left the educational system.[1] Those who stay want something better out of life, and they view a high school diploma as the first among dozens of steps they need to take to reach their dreams. Still, a major hurdle is the high school basic skills exit exam. This chapter details some of what I do as the teacher of what some kids have called "Last Chance English." While it is true that this class prepares students to pass the high school exit exam, the increase in reading and literacy skills that result will serve them far beyond their teenage years.

They have also turned off to all reading because they have not experienced success no matter how hard they have worked. These students bring rich personal stories, but when placed in an academic setting, when competing with other students of their own age group, they simply turn off and shut down.

Because forty to forty-five students are commonly enrolled in these classes, class time is carefully structured to balance reading, writing, listening, and speaking activities, as well as individual, group, and whole-class activities. Table 5.1 provides a summary of the activities I use most frequently and with the greatest success.

Community Building

Literacy experts recognize the importance of creating a physically and emotionally safe classroom environment for all students, but especially for those we label as at-risk (Allen, 1995; Alvermann & Phelps, 1998; Canfield & Wells, 1994). At the beginning of the year, or at any time when several new students are added to the class, I spend two or three days building or reinforcing a student reading and writing community. This is particularly valuable in a class where the students have few opportunities to know others outside their own language or friend groups. One of the most successful of these community-building activities begins when I ask students to make a list of ten of their favorite objects. Students then gather in groups of three where they take turns introducing themselves and naming their ten objects. They listen for matches and compare lists until they have found at least five matching objects. I both join in and monitor this noisy but effective activity. When students can't find matches, they may add another five or ten objects to their lists until they do have a match with at least two others. Canfield and Wells's *100 Ways to Enhance Self-Concept in the Classroom* (1994) and Kirby and Liner's *Inside Out: Developmental Strategies for Teaching Writing* (1988) are excellent resources for other community-building activities. Some instructors may question the time devoted to such activities in my senior classes, but I find these a crucial foundation for all other activities.

Read-alouds

Even though they are seniors in high school, often have jobs, and may have their own children at home, I read aloud frequently to these students. Before I begin, I usually ask an open question about an issue that will arise in the reading, or have students attempt to solve a problem that I describe and that is related to a dilemma in the reading. Such prereading activities oc-

Table 5.1. Key Class Activities

Activity	Modality	Format
Community Building	speaking, listening	whole class
Read-alouds	listening	whole class
Reciprocal Reading	speaking, listening, reading, writing	small group
Learning Reflections	speaking, listening	small group, whole class
Silent Reading	reading	individual
Timed Readings	reading, speaking, listening, calculating	individual
Word and Vocabulary Games	varies	individual, small group
Pumped Up Grammar/ Daily Journal	speaking, listening, reading, writing	individual

cupy little time but pique students' interest. Reading aloud allows my students of all backgrounds to hear English being read by a fluent reader. I sometimes stop briefly during the reading if students wish to clarify something they don't understand or to ask them to make predictions. Sometimes I will read something twice if they didn't quite comprehend with the first reading. At the beginning of the year, the read-alouds are completed in about ten minutes, to match the attention span of my students. Soon, however, I find myself reading for longer periods as these young adults become accustomed to careful listening and get caught up in the magic of story.

The English language evolved from an oral tradition in which gifted storytellers were highly valued, and today storytelling through read-alouds serves an important function in my classroom. Reading aloud helps students visualize characters, places, and events with a detail they might not have been able to imagine if they had read for themselves, when they get bogged down in difficult vocabulary or complex sentence structures. My inflections, pauses, and pronunciations can also provide important clues for my students. Subtle meanings and innuendoes they would likely miss in silent reading come alive in the read-aloud, and students become aware that reading involves the discovery of such meaning, not simply the recognition of words on a page. Also significant is the fact that my reading is nonthreatening to the students. Sadly, some students tell me that such nonthreatening time in an English class is an entirely new experience.

Janet Allen explains about read-alouds:

> [W]e have to be able to bring all of the elements and emotions of the story to life. This is easier to do if the story is one with which the reader personally connects. I know from experience that I can't do this [read with expression] unless I am reading a book I have really enjoyed. (1995, p. 62)

So I choose selections for read-alouds from books such as Maya Angelou's *Wouldn't Take Nothing for My Journey Now* (1997) or Donald Sobol's *Two-Minute Mysteries.* Another excellent resource is *Read All about It!*, edited by Jim Trelease (1993). A variety of other short stories and selections from books and biographies that I also enjoy have proven successful with my students.

Reciprocal Reading

The activity I label "reciprocal reading" plays a central part in the improvements my students make over the course of the year. In reciprocal reading, each small group of students is given a short selection to read. This may be an entire work or a portion of a longer piece. They may take turns reading aloud, read aloud together (chorally), or read silently first and then reread aloud in some fashion. The only assistance I provide, and this is only for more difficult selections, is an introductory open-ended question for discussion or a quick prereading vocabulary lesson on a central word. Otherwise, the group reads and together negotiates the meaning. The group also decides how to complete the reciprocal reading graphic organizer I provide, dividing the work and determining when each aspect should be completed. This group activity places responsibility for genuine comprehension squarely with the students, without teacher assistance, and yet with some structure and the safety net of the group. Students also learn control of their own reading processes, including the value of summarizing, illustrating (or "seeing"), defining vocabulary from context, questioning, and other reading skills (Alvermann & Phelps, 1998). Sometimes the group reading selections vary from group to group, and sometimes they are the same; additionally, the graphic organizer can be modified according to class needs, the demands of particular selections, or even time constraints. Figures 5.1 and 5.2 show graphic organizers I have used with fiction and nonfiction selections.

Learning Reflections

Some of the best moments in these classes result from the kids telling me what we did and what they learned that day. Learning Reflection time occurs daily in my classes, and as the end of the class period approaches, the students will remind me and protest if we run short of time. On occasion, when we carry these reflections over to the first activity of the following day, the day's wait has the added benefit of allowing students to think about their learning for a longer period of time. Most of these students tell me that they have rarely, if ever, been asked to think about and articulate what they have learned: what is relatively easy, what is particularly challenging, what is new, what is review, what is understood, what is understood only partially, or the like. To think about and recognize these facets of learning is an important metacognitive skill, one that good readers practice routinely (Claggett, 1996). By providing the opportunity for reflection on their learning, students gradually and steadily improve in their ability to do so. Students' speaking vocabulary is also extended in new directions as they make these explanations and practice using new vocabulary learned in class. Finally, Learning Reflections allow students to realize they are learning, an accomplishment that needs public and ongoing recognition.

Predictions based on first paragraph	Summary of the story
1	2
3	4
New vocabulary words & meaning guesses	Illustration of key story scene

Figure 5.1. Reciprocal Reading Graphic Organizer: Fiction

Predictions based on title and section heading(s)	Three interesting and new pieces of information
1	2
3	4
Three questions important for the group to discuss to show understanding of the reading (and to ask other groups later)	Three things about the topic that are not explained in the reading that we'd like to know more about

Figure 5.2. Reciprocal Reading Graphic Organizer: Nonfiction

Silent Reading

Students also read silently for twenty to thirty minutes of most class sessions. After establishing this routine over several weeks, I add follow-up discussion so that students begin to talk about what they are reading and what they think about the reading selections. I share what I'm reading, too, modeling possible ways to talk about books. Most of my students are surprised to hear that I'm not sitting around reading Shakespeare all day, a conception of English teachers they seem to hold dear. Instead, I'm candid and ready to share what I'm reading and why I respond to events and characters as I do. Once they realize I will not negatively judge them and their book choices, students freely share their responses to current reading. My top priority is and always has been to open a door for my students: those who don't do much reading or sharing at the beginning of the year usually come around by the end of the year. Some may speak in less than perfect English, but they are trying to self-correct themselves by the end of the year, even when speaking English with those from their own language backgrounds.

When I first began using silent reading time as a staple in my classes, I had meager resources to buy books. So I tried Janet Allen's suggestion of gathering books from my students. For years I had heard people say that "poor" kids have little reading material available to them, but this was simply not true of the students in these classes. I gathered many books from students by offering extra credit to anyone who brought books appropriate for sharing to my classroom. I also accepted *Teen Magazine, Sports Illustrated, People,* and other magazines to which they seem to have ready access. Their homes have magazines and books, and if they aren't filled with books, my students are resourceful enough to go to yard sales, library handout sales, and our own school book depository giveaway days. When he arrived with an armload of books, I asked one student, a two-hundred-pound wrestler, "Who reads all these books?" His answer was remarkably revealing. "Nobody," he said. "My mom wants me to read them, but I just fake it. I wouldn't choose these kinds of books for myself." But somebody else in the class *was* interested in those books. If the books disappear, I suffer no monetary loss, and most of the time they reappear. My philosophy on classroom library books is that if they disappear they must have been good enough for one of my students to read. And, of course, there are other ways to build a classroom library: requesting donations from local businesses or the Parent-Teacher-Student organization, using Title I or other appropriate school monies, or writing grants to funding agencies. I find that a wide variety of materials—mysteries, romances, poetry, science fiction, children's books, magazines—fills the reading needs of my students very nicely. Choice is a crucial element.

Timed Readings

Timed readings are important because "[f]aster readers comprehend faster. . . . Faster readers concentrate better" (Spargo, 1989). My students have rarely been asked to push their reading speed. While they honestly want to read more, they get hung up on individual words or word-by-word reading. Timed readings, used on occasion in a game-like way, help encourage students to read in groups of words and to build their reading speed, even if only a little. I use timed readings once or twice a week and structure them in two different ways, both requiring about twenty minutes of class time. In the first approach, students read for a set amount of time from a short selection I have chosen, perhaps from a book such as *Chicken Soup for the Teenage Soul II* (Canfield, Hansen, & Kirberger, 1998). Early in the year, the time may be a mere two minutes, but we build over the semester to five and ten minutes. When the time elapses, my timer bell rings. Then I ask students to summarize or describe what they read by writing a short paragraph. Sometimes I give feedback on these paragraphs and sometimes class members provide the feedback.

The other method for timed reading is to use selections from a workbook of timed reading passages. These workbooks are available through educational supply stores for a variety of reading levels, and comprehension questions usually accompany each passage. These books also provide reading-speed graphs and a corresponding accuracy graph. Over the course of the year, students do increase their speed and comprehension. They enjoy watching the lines on the graphs edge upward, and they gain self-esteem from their reading abilities. As so many have noted, reading practice, in this case practice reading more quickly, leads to greater reading fluency (Allen, 1995; McQuillan et al., Chapter 6 of this volume).

Word and Vocabulary Games

Word recognition and spelling are ongoing challenges to these students, so brief activities or games focusing on decoding are also ongoing in my classes. My main sources for decoding activities are Eisiminger's *Wordspinner* (1991) and Bear, Templeton, and Invernizzi's *Words Their Way* (1996). For example, many of these students, including the second-language learners, have problems quickly decoding or spelling words with vowel combinations and consonant blends. I create, or have students create, a selection of individual words on index cards with selected vowel combinations or consonant blends. Students then sort and match the cards according to the pronunciations of the vowels or consonants. Vowel sound matches might be "bear" and "fair," "burn" and "curl," or "boil" and "toy." With regular reviews, and as the number of index cards increases, it is amazing how students' decoding and spelling improve.

Students also study vocabulary on a regular basis. I provide them with short lists of key words from the readings they will do in class, including one- or two-sentence contexts. Students attempt to guess the meaning of the identified word from the surrounding context and play games that require them to change the tense or create other forms of the word, write their own sentences, or provide examples (or even nonexamples) of words. Dictionaries are used as a last resort because my students rarely understand the definitions. One of my students' greatest weaknesses as readers is their limited vocabularies. By regularly working on and reviewing vocabulary in enjoyable ways, students' vocabularies improve, along with their potential for reading success.

Pumped Up Grammar

Last in this chapter, but often first on my daily agenda, is the *Pumped Up Grammar* exercise students complete several times a week (Robinson, 1998). I have run hot and cold on "grammar" for a number of years, but the backgrounds and reading weaknesses of my students warrant another look at punctuation, conventions, and the way our language is put together. Besides, a common vocabulary facilitates our discussions of language, writing, and reading. Students write the *Pumped Up Grammar* exercises in a journal that I collect at the end of a week. I make every attempt to focus this activity, keep it brief, and avoid any semblance of intimidation. For example, students might have one minute to write as much as they can, using either *gorilla* or *Uncle Fred* in their writing, one a common noun and the other a proper noun. Or students might be asked to provide in five minutes as many examples as they can of sentences with both direct and indirect objects. I don't dwell on these lessons, but I do ask for immediate examples in order to receive feedback on students' understanding. Reading the student journals at the end of a week also provides feedback on learning. Student feedback has taught me that some parts of speech and punctuation require longer amounts of time to learn than others. Verbs are particularly troublesome for my students, as are plural nouns, possessive nouns, and plural possessives. As a result, I break lessons about such topics into small increments that extend over several weeks and we review regularly. Because I see the results over time in students' writing and class discussions, and because part of the exit exam focuses on these topics, the language lessons are a proven part of the activities in my reading classes for these senior struggling readers.

Conclusion

One key to the success of my students in these classes has been my willingness to stay flexible and change directions frequently. If I find my students stumbling or becoming bored, I change what we're doing immediately. Boredom and stress are the enemies in my classroom. My students have rarely experienced success in school, at least in English. These students may be borderline graduates, but if they stay into their senior year, they are individuals with goals and expectations for themselves. They can be hard workers when they decide they like what they are doing and when they realize that what they are doing is valuable. Achieving that first level of enjoyment and accomplishment takes about two months for these students because so much of their past experience has involved frustration and negative feedback.

The other key to my students' success is that I treat them with respect and as individuals, and I make myself available as a human being. Students don't like me to raise my voice, they tell me, but they do respond when I laugh or poke fun at myself. I try not to single out individuals unless they want or demand the spotlight. I set a fast pace, plan highly structured classes, and set high standards and expectations. In the end, these students seem to want to know me, to make a human connection with an adult. They listen attentively to the stories I tell and read, some poignant, some exhilarating, some not so heroic. Through these stories, the stories they read, and the class activities, many students become actively involved with learning, able not only to graduate from high school, but also to walk through doors to new opportunities in their lives.

Note

1. Since this chapter was written, a program has been implemented to assist students in making the transition to high school and to promote their staying in school.

References

Allen, J. (1995). *It's never too late: Leading adolescents to lifelong literacy.* Portsmouth, NH: Heinemann.

Alvermann, D. E., & Phelps, S. F. (1998). *Content reading and literacy: Succeeding in today's diverse classrooms* (2nd ed.). Boston: Allyn & Bacon.

Angelou, M. (1997). *Wouldn't take nothing for my journey now.* New York: Bantam Books.

Bear, D., Templeton, S., & Invernizzi, M. (1996). *Words their way: Word study for phonics, vocabulary, and spelling.* Upper Saddle River, NJ: Merrill.

Canfield, J., Hansen, M. V., & Kirberger, K. (1998). *Chicken soup for the teenage soul II.* Deerfield Beach, FL: Heath Communications.

Canfield, J., and Wells, H. C. (1994). *100 ways to enhance self-concept in the classroom: A handbook for teachers, counselors, and group leaders* (2nd ed.). Boston: Allyn & Bacon.

Claggett, F. (1996). *A measure of success: From assignment to assessment in English language arts.* Portsmouth, NH: Boynton/Cook.

Eisiminger, S. (1991). *Wordspinner: Mind-boggling games for word lovers.* Savage, MD: Littlefield Adams.

Kirby, D., & Liner, T., with Vinz, R. (1988). *Inside out: Developmental strategies for teaching writing* (2nd ed.). Portsmouth, NH: Boynton/Cook.

Robinson, R. L. (1998). *Daily doses of pumped up grammar.* Poway, CA: Twin Peaks Middle School.

Sobol, D. J. (1967). *Two-minute mysteries.* New York: Scholastic.

Spargo, E. (Ed.). (1989). *Timed readings in literature: Fifty 400-word passages with questions for building reading speed.* Chicago, IL: Jamestown.

Trelease, J. (Ed.). (1993). *Read all about it! Great read-aloud stories, poems, and newspaper pieces for preteens and teens.* New York: Penguin Books.

6 If You Build It, They Will Come: A Book Flood Program for Struggling Readers in an Urban High School

Jeff McQuillan
California State University, Fullerton

with

**Jeannie Beckett, Lupe Gutierrez, Matthew Rippon,
Sue Snyder, Doug Wager, Gregg Williams, and Eydie Zajec**
Sequoyah Scholars Program, Anaheim High School, California

While the focus on recent reading initiatives has been on "early intervention" in the primary grades, there are thousands of older struggling readers for whom such programs are clearly of no benefit (Krashen & McQuillan, 1996). Students who are already in middle school, junior high, or high school and are still not proficient readers need instead "late" intervention in order to "catch up" to their age peers in reading. Research has shown that rapid progress in reading is possible if students are exposed to a rich source of reading materials and given the opportunity to read books that are both interesting and comprehensible (Krashen & McQuillan, 1996; McQuillan, 1997a). In this chapter, we describe the implementation and initial results of one such late intervention effort, the Sequoyah Scholars "book flood" program at Anaheim High School in Anaheim, California.

A Diverse, Urban Setting: Anaheim High School

Anaheim High School (AHS) is typical of many urban secondary schools with low-achieving students. The majority of its 2,400 students participate in federally funded free or reduced-cost lunch programs,

and nearly half (48 percent) are designated as limited English proficient (LEP), the vast majority from Spanish-language households. The
school is situated in a largely working-class area of Anaheim, in the
shadow of well-known tourist attractions such as Disneyland and
Knott's Berry Farm. English classes at the school are tracked, resulting
in a small group of honors and university prep students, and a much
larger group of "regular" and Title I/remedial students. In the spring
1998 administration of the Stanford 9 test, 68 percent of the school's
ninth graders scored below the 25th percentile on the Total Reading
subsection. Virtually all of the students in the Title I program scored
below the bottom quartile. That same spring, only one-third of the
ninth graders at AHS met the district's standard of a 2.0 GPA, and most
of these were in the honors and university prep classes.

Under the leadership of site coordinator Jeannie Beckett, in 1998
the Title I reading teachers at AHS created the Sequoyah Scholars program for the approximately 420 students served by the school's Title I
grant. The demographics of the Title I students match those of the
school as a whole: 92 percent are Latino/Hispanic; about half are LEP.
Fewer than ten of those served by the program are identified as special
education students. Students in the reading component of the program
are placed at one of three levels:

- **Advanced English Language Development (ELD)** Students
  who are limited English proficient and who received core curriculum equivalent to English I. Students are at a variety of
  age/grade levels from 9–12.

- **English I/Reading Improvement:** English-only students and
  those who have been redesignated or initially determined to
  be fluent English proficient.

- **English II:** Students who successfully completed either Advanced ELD or English I.

Students in Advanced ELD and English I/Reading Improvement receive instruction in two-hour blocks each day. English II students have a
typical single class period daily. Identified ninth-grade students receive
a letter in the summer notifying them that they have been selected to
participate in this special program, and follow-up phone calls are made
to parents. The overall program has several components, including a
parent institute, field trips, a computer writing lab, tutoring, and support services provided by a bilingual (Spanish/English) paraprofes-
sional and the program coordinator. Five teachers form the core team of
instructors for the program, and they meet regularly to discuss students
and curricular implementation.

The Problem: Students Who Don't Read Much (and Don't Have Much to Read)

Teachers in the Sequoyah Scholars program are committed to the idea that the primary goal of Title I intervention is to increase the amount that students read. Underlying this goal are the beliefs that, as Smith (1994) has stated, we "learn to read by reading," that students who read more will become better readers, and that better reading will be reflected in all areas of literacy, including writing competency. These beliefs are founded on considerable research, which has shown that more reading does indeed lead to better reading among students of all ages (Krashen, 1993; McQuillan, 1998). In addition, the program embraces the notion that the amount of reading students do, particularly pleasure or "free voluntary" reading, is closely related to the ready availability of books in students' environments. *Students who have greater access to books will tend to read more.* Again, these beliefs are based on considerable research (Krashen, 1993; McQuillan, 1998; Elley, 1991, 1992).

Consistent with this research, the struggling students selected for the Sequoyah Scholars program state that they almost never read for pleasure and have relatively restricted access to books. In one-on-one, teacher-student conferences in the fall, students reflect mostly negative attitudes toward reading and report little reading outside of school. Students in the program also have significantly fewer books at home, only about one-third the number reported in the average U.S. home for high school students. As shown in Figure 6.1, ninth-grade students in the Sequoyah program report having just over 50 books in their homes (mean = 50.89, standard deviation = 71.20), substantially below the national average of 137 (Elley, 1992). These figures include all books in the home (cookbooks, the Bible, etc.), not just those owned or read by the student. In addition, some of these books are probably in a language other than English, since many students come from Spanish-speaking homes. In terms of access to English-language reading materials, then, these urban Title I students are at a distinct disadvantage compared to the average U.S. high schooler.

School does not level the playing field. Anaheim High School has a books-per-pupil ratio of around 8:1, compared to the national average for high schools of 19:1 (White, 1990). These numbers are comparable to other urban schools and reflect the general disparity between urban and advantaged suburban communities in literacy resources (Allington, Guice, Baker, Michaelson, & Li, 1995; Di Loreto & Tse, 1999; McQuillan, 1998; Smith, Constantino, & Krashen, 1997). This is why increased access to reading materials is a central goal of the Title I Sequoyah Scholars program.

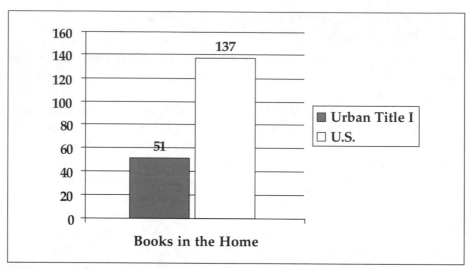

Figure 6.1. Number of Books at Home of Urban Title I Students and U.S. Average

The Sequoyah Scholars Program:
Eight Steps to Success

In reviewing the research literature on successful sustained silent reading (SSR) programs, Pilgreen and Gribbons (1998) note eight characteristics of a good "book flood" program for elementary and secondary schools. The Sequoyah Scholars teachers worked to put all eight in place.

Staff Development

Key to beginning any new program is getting the commitment and involvement of the critical players—the teachers themselves. This step should not be overlooked. If teachers are not "on board," little change will take place in the classroom. In the Sequoyah Scholars program, the five Title I reading teachers met on a monthly basis to discuss the progress of the SSR component, including problems with book access, what to do with students who did not participate, types of materials to allow, and so forth. They read about successful programs, participated in regular inservice sessions by local university faculty on setting up free reading programs, and reflected on their own experiences in the classroom. All of these activities were crucial in forming a sense of unified purpose and solving problems that arose.

Appealing Books at the Student's Reading Level

Many of the Sequoyah Scholars were used to feeling frustrated when attempting to read assigned texts that were too difficult for them or held little personal interest. The teachers decided to ensure that the books available to students were both appealing and comprehensible. This was no easy task, since the books that students could read were often not interesting, and the books that were interesting were many times too difficult for them. Teachers experimented with various types of books, relying on student surveys, recommended reading lists of adolescent literature, and trial and error. Following is a partial list of some of the books teachers nominated as "favorites" in terms of popularity, as well as books that appeared frequently on student reading logs. Surprisingly, many of the "junior high" level series books (e.g., the *Goosebumps* series by R. L. Stine) were quite popular with students, but so too were books that were generally well-liked by other high school students (e.g., *Chicken Soup for the Teenage Soul*). Popular authors included Dean Koontz, Stephen King, Caroline Cooney, Will Hobbs, Paul Zindel, Cynthia Voight, Walter Dean Myers, David Klass, and Joan Lowery Nixon, among others.

> *Among Friends,* Caroline Cooney
> *The Black Pearl,* Scott O'Dell
> *The Boy Who Drank Too Much,* Shep Greene
> *Chicken Soup for the Teenage Soul,* Jack Canfield
> *The Color Purple,* Alice Walker
> *The Crossing,* Gary Paulsen
> *The Duplicate,* William Sleator
> *The Firm,* John Grisham
> *Go Ask Alice,* Anonymous
> *Goosebumps* series, R. L. Stine
> *Guinness Book of World Records*
> *Hatchet,* Gary Paulsen
> *Icebound,* Dean Koontz
> *I Do,* Elizabeth Chandler
> *I Know What You Did Last Summer,* Lois Duncan
> *Island of the Blue Dolphins,* Scott O'Dell
> *The Lion, the Witch, and the Wardrobe,* C. S. Lewis
> *Maniac Magee,* Jerry Spinelli

Maus I & II, Art Spiegelman

Melody, V. C. Andrews

Off and Running, Gary Soto

Roswell High series, Melinda Metz (e.g., *The Wild One*)

The Secret Garden, Frances Hodgson Burnett

Sometimes I Think I Hear My Name, Avi

Sports and Entertainment Autobiographies (e.g., Michael Jordan, Sammy Sosa, Selena)

Starring Sally J. Freedman as Herself, Judy Blume

Stephen King novels

Stone Fox, John Reynolds Gardner

Stranger with My Face, Lois Duncan

Superfudge, Judy Blume

Sweet Valley Saga series, Francine Pascal

That Was Then, This Is Now, S. E. Hinton

Top Wing, Matt Christopher

True Story Biographies

Where the Red Fern Grows, Wilson Rawls

Direct, Easy Access to Books

When the Sequoyah program first began, students came to class without any free reading materials for SSR time. When taken to the school library during the beginning of the year, several students confessed to feeling overwhelmed by the number of choices available to them, and they had little idea how to find the books they wanted. To overcome this hurdle, the teachers decided to set up a classroom library in each of their classrooms. The purpose of the libraries was twofold: first, to provide students who were intimidated by the regular school or public library with a smaller but focused group of books, and second, to give students who "forgot" their book easy and direct access to reading materials. Classroom libraries began with 50 to 200 books, but by the end of the year, each class had between 150 and 400 books for each of the twenty to thirty-five students in the classes. Even this number was probably not sufficient, however. As students became more interested in reading, the demand for books increased. In Gregg Williams's class, students had folders in which they could keep their books, if they chose to. Several students were found to be stockpiling the "good" books, placing three or four books in their folders to make sure they were available when they were ready to read them.

The classroom libraries also provided books not found in the school library and were set up to display popular titles in an inviting way (with the cover facing out). The libraries thus served very effectively as "ads" for reading, surrounding students with reading materials. Most of the classroom libraries contained only books, not magazines or comics. There was some discussion during the monthly teacher planning days about whether this was a good thing, but the majority of the teachers believed that books provided high school students with more "carry over" reading outside of class. Almost all students did, in fact, take to reading books once the program was underway.

Time to Read

Fundamental to any SSR program is, of course, a set amount of time *each day* for students to read to themselves. Pilgreen and Gribbons (1998) point out that successful SSR programs must be carried out on a regular and frequent basis and not as an occasional activity or tacked on as "filler" on Friday. The teachers started off slowly, allotting ten minutes a day during the first few weeks of the semester. Most students weren't accustomed to having time for pleasure reading in class, and some needed to work into the habit gradually. No other reading materials (e.g., textbooks) were allowed, and students were not permitted to work on homework or class assignments. Within four to six weeks, the time spent reading was gradually increased to fifteen and then twenty minutes. Several teachers noted that many students can sit, do nothing, and avoid reading for ten minutes, but when the SSR is twenty minutes, it is almost impossible for students to do nothing. At that point, they start reading. In some classes, students would read thirty minutes, complaining if they were given less time! Teachers report that 90 to 95 percent of their students were, in fact, reading their books, consistent with other reports that have found that, when properly implemented, almost all students take advantage of the SSR time provided (Cohen, 1999; Von Sprecken & Krashen, 1998).

> *Several teachers noted that many students can sit, do nothing, and avoid reading for ten minutes, but when the SSR is twenty minutes, it is almost impossible for students to do nothing. At that point, they start reading.*

Conducive Environment

Pilgreen and Gribbons (1998) note that an environment "conducive" to SSR does not necessarily require soft pillows and plush carpet.

Instead, teachers can make students comfortable by setting up a structure in which they are free to take risks. This means allowing students to abandon books they dislike, read at their own pace, and be free of disruptions and distractions. SSR time in the Sequoyah Scholars program is considered "sacred time"—nothing is allowed to interfere with it. Several teachers have noted that when a visitor comes to the door, or an announcement comes on over the PA, students audibly groan. This is how it should be: Nothing should be allowed to distract students from their reading. During midyear conferences, several students will always comment that what they like most about SSR time is the peace and quiet created by a roomful of people reading. Some say it is the only part of their day that is relaxing and enjoyable. The Sequoyah Scholar students, many of whom "hate" to read at the beginning of the year, become thoroughly enthralled by their daily reading. Gregg Williams reports that in one of his classes, a student got up to answer the door for a visitor during SSR time. She was so involved in her book that she continued reading as she walked toward the door, feeling her way along the wall with one hand!

Teacher Encouragement

A key way for teachers to encourage reading is by setting an example: *Teachers must always participate in SSR as readers themselves.* This point cannot be overemphasized. The teacher serves as an important role model in reading for the students. When the teacher takes attendance or works on other matters instead of reading, students get the message that reading is not valued. Indeed, several of the teachers observed that when they were interrupted by a call or message at the classroom door, many students simply stopped reading. This is consistent with research by Von Sprecken and Krashen (1998), who found the participation of the teacher in the SSR time a key predictor of whether students were actually reading in their classes.

Of course, teachers do other things to promote reading. One of the most successful strategies is recommending books to students. Teachers often do "book talks"—brief reviews of books—on new additions to their classroom libraries, or talk about a book they are reading themselves. Without fail, the promoted book disappears from the teacher's desk minutes after the talk is over. Students are also encouraged to share what they are reading with their classmates during book talk time. Again, these results are consistent with other research, which has found that low-achieving students rely heavily on teachers for their reading recommendations (Fleener, Morrison, Linek, & Rasinski, 1997).

Doug Wager notes that "book talks are one of the most powerful tools I've come across to encourage students to read something they may have passed up." Wager notes that his book talks take many forms:

> One time when I was reading *Shoeless Joe* I simply mentioned that I was really enjoying the book at the end of the reading period. A student saw the cover of the book and asked me if it was about baseball. I told him, "Yes and no." Without planning on it, I spent the next few minutes telling about the book. By the time I finished talking there were three students vying for the right to read the only copy when I was done. I'm not sure any student had read it before that point.

Other times, Wager uses a more systematic approach, such as when he has just purchased several new books for his classroom library. Bringing the books into class in a large shopping bag, he pulls them out one by one to talk about them, heightening the students' interest.

> I'll give brief book talks on just about all the new books we're adding. Sometimes all I'll do is read the title, author, and the back cover. . . . Generally, I spend no more than thirty seconds or so in this situation on each book. Yet these can be quite powerful. The first time I did this, the class rushed to grab the books when I was done.

Based on several years of using book talks in his classroom, Gregg Williams makes the following recommendations:

- Be enthusiastic while giving the book talk. An attitude that says, "You really need to read this book!" is important.

- While giving the talk, walk around the room showing students the cover, and mention the author and title more than once.

- Select a variety of genres to talk about over the course of the semester or year.

- Pick books that you have read before. If you haven't read the book, then talk about what you have heard others say about it, and read the back cover with enthusiasm.

- Talk about books that have been read and highly recommended by former students. Students often value their peers' opinions more than their teachers'.

- Mention other titles by the author of the current book you're promoting. Like many readers, students enjoy reading "series" books and works by the same author.

- Be sure to give book talks at the beginning of the school year to "hook" students. Book talks can also serve as something of a pep talk on what books are currently in the classroom library.
- Try to obtain more than one copy of the books you choose for your book talks. Invariably, more than one student will want to read it after you've built it up.
- Have students stamp new books with the school property stamp and cover them in clear plastic to guard against wear and tear. This process gets students handling and flipping through all of the new acquisitions, further piquing their interest.

Teachers also reach out to parents to promote reading. Lupe Gutierrez taught a weekly English as a Second Language class for parents of Title I students. She displayed her students' favorite books in front of the classroom and talked to the parents about what students were reading. She emphasized how important it was for them to encourage their children to read at home.

No Accountability

No grades or rewards are attached to students' reading during SSR time. Such rewards have been found to be ineffective in promoting reading achievement or positive motivation to read (McQuillan, 1997). Instead, in the Sequoyah Scholars program, reading is considered its own reward. Students who do not participate initially are encouraged to read during SSR time, and by the end of the first six weeks, almost all students are actively reading books with little or no prompting from their teacher.

Follow-up Activities

Students engage in some nongraded follow-up activities related to their reading, but these are quite minimal. In some classes, students are asked to write a short reflection (not a synopsis) on what they have read that day. In most classes, students simply record the author and title of the books they have read as they finish them (or abandon them). Teachers encourage students to talk about their books amongst themselves, and provide time for students to share with the entire class something about the books they are reading.

Lost in the Book Flood

A critical component of the Sequoyah Scholars program is increasing students' access to interesting and comprehensible reading materials. As noted earlier, at the beginning of the program most classroom libraries began with a small number of books (usually less than fifty). In late November and again in early February, the teachers used Title I funds to purchase books for their classrooms. They began their task by polling the students, asking each one to pick out a book they wanted to see added to their classroom library. That list was supplemented by some "recommended reading lists" found in Nancie Atwell's *In the Middle* (1998) and other sources (e.g., *The Journal of Adolescent and Adult Literacy*).

The reaction of the students to this new infusion of books was nothing less than spectacular: Sue Snyder found students lined up at her door a half hour before school began, wanting to get a look at the new books! "Did you bring our new books?"; "Did you get the one I ordered?"; "Can I take this one home?" These were the same students who, only a few months earlier, had considered themselves nonreaders. Teachers took class time to give a brief synopsis of each new book they had purchased. During the next few days, Eydie Zajec's students even stayed in the classroom during their breaks to examine all the new books and to make their selections. By the end of the first day with the new books, most were checked out and being devoured by this group of "remedial" readers. Doug Wager reported that after bringing in his new books, "I was overrun by a mob of fourteen-year-olds fighting over books. Books!"

No grade-level markings are put on the books, as is popular in some computerized book management programs. Students simply browse through the books and determine if they like the book and are able to read it. Teachers report no problems with students finding books they can understand and enjoy. The teachers do make recommendations to particular students about the kinds of books they think the student might enjoy, including books that are more "advanced" in reading difficulty than the student's current selections. But students are free to accept or reject any recommendation and to abandon books they don't find interesting.

The Results: More Books, More Reading, Better Reading

The most powerful indications of the success of the book flood program are the reactions of the students themselves. The teachers report that most of the students begin the semester with a negative view of reading. By the end of the first semester, almost all of them have read several books on their own, and continue to read throughout the school year. Teachers meet with the students three times over the course of the year in one-on-one conferences, and they can see the progress their students have made in the depth and breadth of reading interests and difficulty.

In the first year of the program, a social science teacher reported that two of the Sequoyah Scholar students were visiting her classroom during lunch one day and were talking about all of the books they had been reading. The teacher's comment to the Sequoyah program teachers was, "You must be doing something right!" On year-end Title I program reviews, every one of the five Seqouyah Scholar teachers named the book flood as the greatest milestone in student progress. They called it the year of "BOOKS, BOOKS, BOOKS!"

At the end of the first year, more formal measures of progress were also taken of vocabulary growth and writing proficiency of a selected subsample of English I students. Sequoyah Scholar students in English I made statistically significant gains in vocabulary, writing fluency, and writing complexity (see McQuillan, 1999, for details). Since the Sequoyah Scholar program included all students at the school targeted for Title I support, there was no way to create a suitable control group of low-achieving students with which to compare these results. As such, they should be viewed only as suggestive. Nevertheless, the results are consistent with other evidence that shows the impact of increased reading on vocabulary development and writing proficiency (see Krashen, 1993, for a review).

Did more reading lead to better reading? To help answer this question, we compared the number of pages students read throughout the year (recorded on their reading logs) with the gains they made in vocabulary. Vocabulary knowledge is strongly related to reading comprehension ability; growth in one is usually an indicator of growth in the other. Students completed a vocabulary recognition test (VRT) in September and then again in May of the 1998–99 school year. The VRT consisted of 96 items, including both real and false words. Students simply checked the words they recognized (the false words were used to correct the scores for guessing). This simple measure has been found to be a good indicator of overall vocabulary knowledge and reading proficiency (Stanovich & Cunningham, 1992). The VRT used here was piloted during the previous school year on a similar group of students, who scored similarly on the VRT and the Stanford 9 Total Reading score.

The correlation between the gains on the VRT and the number of pages students reported reading during the school year was positive and statistically significant.[1] This suggests that the more students read, the higher their gains in vocabulary, a finding consistent with experimental evidence on the effects of increased reading on literacy development (Krashen, 1993). An additional analysis, this time using the spring and fall VRT scores, confirmed the previous result that the number of pages students read was a significant predictor of their vocabulary score, regardless of previous vocabulary knowledge (McQuillan, 1999). Similar conclusions were reached by Anderson, Wilson, and Fielding (1988) in their study of middle school readers—that is, more leisure reading is associated with better reading proficiency.

Conclusions

The Sequoyah Scholars program is unique in offering low-achieving high school readers an opportunity often denied them in school: to read for pleasure (Allington, 1980). Teachers in the program work hard to establish a classroom climate that encourages reading in a variety of ways—through time, encouragement, and resources. Establishing such a program demands the commitment of both teachers and school administrators to staff development, a plentiful supply of books, and a dedicated time for free reading. Most important, book flood and SSR programs provide tangible evidence that "just reading" is, in fact, one of the most powerful curricular interventions we can provide for low-achieving students.

Epilogue: The Success Goes On . . . and On

Three years after the Sequoyah Scholars project was begun, it continues to have a positive impact on reading achievement and motivation among AHS students. The second and third years of the program were even more successful than the first—teachers reported that the students' reading fluency, comprehension, and enjoyment continued to grow. Gregg Williams's tenth graders who "graduated" from the program after its first year even came back throughout the following years, asking if they could borrow books from his classroom library. New ninth graders took to reading as their peers had the previous years, and more books were continuously added to the classroom libraries.

At the end of the second and third years of the program, both the ninth- and tenth-grade Sequoyah Scholars went on a "book spree" to a local bookstore, an event that only the ninth graders had attended during the first year of the program. Each student was sponsored by a member of the community, receiving fifteen dollars to purchase a book of his or her own. The results of the trip were amazing: the "veteran" students were showing the ninth graders around the store; for some students, this was the first book they had ever purchased on their own. Thanks to the book flood approach, students once labeled nonreaders were continuing to read.

Note

1. $r = .40$, $N = 31$, $p < .05$. Multiple regression analysis also indicated that the number of pages read was a significant predictor of vocabulary gain scores over the school year, controlling for reading proficiency as measured by the previous year's Stanford 9 Total Reading score.

References

Allington, R. (1980). Poor readers don't get to read much in reading groups. *Language Arts, 57*, 872–76.

Allington, R., Guice, S., Baker, K., Michaelson, N., & Li, S. (1995). Access to books: Variations in schools and classrooms. *Language and Literacy Spectrum, 5*, 23–25.

Anderson, R., Wilson, P., & Fielding, L. (1988). Growth in reading and how children spend their time outside of school. *Reading Research Quarterly, 23*, 285–303.

Atwell, N. (1998). *In the middle: New understandings about writing, reading, and learning* (2nd ed.). Portsmouth, NH: Boynton/Cook.

Cohen, K. (1999). Reluctant eighth grade readers enjoy sustained silent reading. *California Reader, 33*(1), 22–24.

Di Loreto, C., & Tse, L. (1999). Seeing is believing: Disparity in books in two Los Angeles area public libraries. *Public Library Quarterly, 17*(3), 31–36.

Elley, W. (1991). Acquiring literacy in a second language: The effect of book-based programs. *Language Learning, 41*, 375–411.

Elley, W. (1992). *How in the world do students read? IEA study of reading literacy.* The Hague, Netherlands: International Association for the Evaluation of Educational Achievement.

Fleener, C., Morrison, S., Linek, W., & Rasinski, T. (1997). Recreational reading choices: How do children select books? In W. Linek & E. Sturtevant (Eds.), *Exploring literacy: The nineteenth annual yearbook of the College Reading Association* (pp. 75–84). Platteville: University of Wisconsin.

Krashen, S. (1993). *The power of reading: Insights from the research.* Englewood, CO: Libraries Unlimited.

Krashen, S., & McQuillan, J. (1996). *The case for late intervention: Once a good reader, always a good reader.* Culver City, CA: Language Education Associates.

McQuillan, J. (1997a). The case of late readers. In P. Dryer (Ed.), *The 61st annual Claremont Reading Conference yearbook* (pp. 48–59). Claremont, CA: Claremont Reading Conference.

McQuillan, J. (1997b). The effects of incentives on reading. *Reading Research and Instruction, 36,* 111–25.

McQuillan, J. (1998). *The literacy crisis: False claims, real solutions.* Portsmouth, NH: Heinemann.

McQuillan, J. (1999). *The effects of a sustained silent reading program on literacy development among low-achieving high school students.* Manuscript in preparation.

Pilgreen, J., & Gribbons, B. (1998). Using SSR in the secondary ESL classroom: A powerful way to increase comprehension and develop positive attitudes toward reading. In R. Constantino (Ed.), *Literacy, access, and libraries among the language minority population* (pp. 127–54). Lanham, MD: Scarecrow Press.

Smith, C., Constantino, R., & Krashen, S. (1997). Differences in print environment for children in Beverly Hills, Compton, & Watts. *Emergency Librarian, 24,* 8–9.

Smith, F. (1994). *Understanding reading: A psycholinguistic analysis of reading and learning to read* (5th ed.). Hillsdale, NJ: Erlbaum.

Stanovich, K., & Cunningham, A. (1992). Studying the consequences of literacy within a literate society: The cognitive correlates of print exposure. *Memory and Cognition, 20,* 51–68.

Von Sprecken, D., & Krashen, S. (1998). Do students read during sustained silent reading? *California Reader, 32*(1), 11–13.

White, H. (1990). School library collections and services: Ranking the states. *School Library Media Quarterly, 19,* 13–26.

7 Students Becoming Real Readers: Literature Circles in High School English Classes

Sandra Okura DaLie
Grant High School, Los Angeles

The most important revelation I have had about what we do as teachers is the realization that learning must be student centered (Brooks & Brooks, 1993). Students, not the teacher, must be at the heart of the learning process, and they must be active participants in their own learning process, not passive recipients. No other idea has influenced me and transformed the way I teach more than this one. The second most influential understanding I have developed is that learning is not neat and tidy, something to be regimented by straight rows, silence, and wrong or right answers. If students are indeed to be active participants in their own learning process, then they must have the opportunity and the freedom to talk, challenge, experiment, and collaborate. Genuine learning is, therefore, a bit messy, unquestionably noisy, often surprising, and always rewarding to observe.

Extending these insights to reading in the high school recently led me to embrace with enthusiasm literature circles. Literature circles provide an opportunity for me to teach the reading of literary text in a way that is consistent with what I understand about learning and reading. For too long we veteran teachers have clung to the archaic notions that we hold all the correct answers, that we are founts of all interpretive wisdom and literary understanding, and that it is our mission to impart all that we know and love of literature to the uninformed and unenlightened. In clinging to these misbeliefs, we have not allowed our students to genuinely make meaning in their reading, nor to discover for themselves the simple joy of reading a good book and talking about it with others. Harvey Daniels recognized that we teachers have "traditionally allowed kids little choice or ownership of their reading, instead marching them through an endless lockstep series of teacher-selected and teacher-controlled readings. . . . The result: kids don't get enough practice with reading to get good at it—or like it" (1994, p. 11). Within the construct of literature circles, however, students select a book they want to read, frame and negotiate meaning, and then talk about it, just like "real" readers.

Literature circles were first introduced by Daniels to colleagues in the Chicago area. The circles are becoming enormously popular among teachers across the country, probably because they are so versatile and can be modified to accommodate a wide range of ages, circumstances, and needs. Still, some basic tenets of literature circles should be emphasized:

- Students choose their own reading materials and form groups based on book choice, with different groups reading different books.
- Groups meet regularly to discuss their reading.
- Students create notes, questions, or drawings to guide their discussion.
- Group discussions should be open and natural, an activity in which personal connections, digressions, fun, imagination, curiosity, and even disagreements are welcome.
- Initially, while learning to interact in literature circles, students assume designated roles with specified tasks.
- The teacher serves as a facilitator only, not as a participant.
- Evaluation is by teacher observation and student self-evaluation.
- When students are finished reading and discussing a book, they form new groups around new reading choices. (Daniels, 1994, p. 18; LiteratureCircles.com, 2000).

How Literature Circles Work

I teach a diverse range of students in a large urban public high school; my classes include everything from Advanced Placement English literature to sheltered first-year classes. I use literature circles with all my students and encounter widely varying reactions. The students who seem to enjoy literature circles the most are the English-language learners, the recent immigrants who have completed the English Language Development (or ESL) course of study and are transitioning to regular English classes. These students are discovering, perhaps for the first time, that their newly acquired reading abilities can be a source of accomplishment and satisfaction. My more able readers (e.g., those identified as honors and gifted kids) need a little help in becoming comfortable with new classroom dynamics because literature circles are a new experience for most. Many of them have been so driven by external incentives such as tests and grades that they are not accustomed to reading for enjoyment or creating their own meaning, at least not in a school setting. And sadly, some of them are more familiar with competition than collaboration and must adapt to cooperative, productive group settings. Among these students, it is gratifying to see real readers emerge from hiding to promote a particular understanding of a character or profess a love and passion for books that heretofore might have seemed "uncool."

I use literature circles for a variety of purposes, in a number of different ways. Admittedly, I have at times used variations of the format to salvage poor time management on my part, as, for example, near the end of the school year when students need to complete several required core readings. I have also used literature circles with a single text for students with limited English proficiency when I felt that my more teacher-centered instruction wasn't getting through to them. But literature circles work best simply as a way to lure my students to read for pleasure, when the main objective is to allow students to read freely, joyfully, and independently.

This is how the process works: For a class size of thirty, I obtain about five copies of six different books. I try to choose books of high interest but varying reading levels to accommodate the range of reading abilities among my students. I preview each book with the entire class. Together, we talk about the title of the book. What do you think it means? We look at the illustrations on the cover. What do you predict will happen in this book? We think about the author. Have you read anything else by this person? Did you like it? After this brief discussion, students get to browse, just like real readers do when they go to a bookstore or library. I allow them time to get up and go to a book, pick it up, weigh it in their hands (an important consideration to a high school student seems to be how heavy a book is), check out the size of the print (another important consideration), and, most important, read the back cover. Students must

> *But literature circles work best simply as a way to lure my students to read for pleasure, when the main objective is to allow students to read freely, joyfully, and independently.*

then write down their first and second choices. I collect these papers and announce the book selections the following day. Ideally, I would let every student have his or her first choice, but I have found the logistics a little easier to manage—e.g., classroom space, number of books—if I even out the groups and keep them to around five people to a book. A student who is frequently absent from class might become the sixth member of a group.

The next day I announce the book assignments and distribute the role description sheets and the timeline. Students form groups according to the books they have been assigned. The first thing the groups must do is "chunk out" their book. Here is math and English interdisciplinary instruction in action. The students determine the number of pages in their book and divide it by the number of literature circle meetings we have scheduled (usually six or eight) to determine the average number of pages they must finish as their outside reading. Students learn to "smooth out" the chunks by flipping pages forward or backward a page or two to find a logical break in the text as a stopping point. This feature of literature circles is in itself a valuable exercise for teenagers learning about responsible time management. Each group then completes a timeline, apprising me of the reading schedule. The process is most likely to break down when students come to class on literature circle days and say they "forgot" what the reading assignment was. Having a copy of the schedule in their notebook seems to have little impact on some students in my classes. Instead, I have found that students prefer to use sticky notes to mark off the chunks of their text rather than write the assignments down in their notebooks. They affix the sticky notes upside down, with about a quarter of an inch protruding from the top of the book. They write the discussion dates on the portions of the notes that protrude.

Next, the students decide on the roles they are to assume during literature circle discussions. There is some debate among my colleagues about the use of assigned roles in literature circles. Ideally, students should engage in book talk freely and without artificial constraints or demands. Successful conversation in groups for my classes, however, requires careful consideration, without which a barrage of questions and complaints would begin: "Chris is just sitting there and not doing any of the work." "Lee is absent again. Will this hurt our group grade?" Assigned literature circle roles provide students with boundaries and clear expectations, and I find that they respond well to this kind of structure. Groups become more productive and the quality of conversation improves. Equally important, these roles have supported all of my students in acquiring the behaviors, skills, and vocabulary of readers.

One way to facilitate the assignment of roles is to distribute a list of the roles with their titles and responsibilities. Daniels created a list of roles that has stood the tests of time and practice (1994, pp. 24–25). I have modified role descriptions slightly for my high school students by writing them as if they were jobs for which they might apply. For each role, I provide a job description, qualifications needed, and the specific responsibilities the job will entail. Here is a sample:

Discussion Director

Job Description	Your job is to develop a list of questions that your group will want to discuss about the reading. Through your questions, you must help people recognize important ideas in the book. You must control the conversation so that everyone has a fair chance to express his or her opinion.
Qualifications	Must have leadership abilities. Also must have a good understanding of the book in order to ask questions that will evoke thoughtful discussion. Must have good attendance.
Responsibilities	You must provide at least five questions at each meeting of your literature circle. You must make sure that everyone in your group has an opportunity to speak.

In describing the specific qualifications needed for each role, I intentionally include some roles for which good attendance is not mandatory. Students with poor attendance are a reality at my school and a challenge to group work. I have found that providing a specific role for this type of student, something like Vocabulary Enricher, is a feasible and humane response to a difficult situation. The diverse literature circle roles allow students to exercise their unique strengths, learning modalities, and intelligences. Students are amazingly adept at choosing appropriate roles for themselves.

I have observed literature circles in action in many different classrooms, and while every teacher has modified the format slightly to suit his or her needs, the roles remain fairly consistent. What varies is the teacher's decision about the length of time a student assumes a role. Some teachers like to have their students rotate roles with every meeting of the literature circle so that ultimately every student has the opportunity to function in every role. My preference is to allow students to stay in their roles through the completion of a book. I find that they get into a groove and become increasingly proficient at their jobs.

One activity teachers can use to introduce literature circles in their classes is whole-class practice with a short story, allowing students to model every role before breaking out into groups. Recently, as an introduction to literature circles I used *Of Mice and Men* with all groups and required every student to create a portfolio of examples of his or her work for each literature circle role. The fine quality of their responses assured me that these students were willing to assume these roles independent of further instruction.

Literature Circle Roles and Responsibilities

The **Discussion Director** creates open-ended questions and facilitates group discussion. Directors must understand that their role is not to "give the right answers" but to promote deep understanding and lively conversation. It is also important to help potential Discussion Directors recognize the kinds of questions they should ask and those they should avoid. After a little practice and modeling, students rise to the challenge and provide fresh insights that often surpass my expectations. For instance, a Discussion Director in charge of a conversation about *Of Mice and Men* asked her group, "Who do you think needed the other person more, George or Lennie?"

Other sample questions:

- What was going through your mind when you read this?
- What are the one or two most important ideas or developments?
- What parts are still unclear to you? Or what didn't you understand about a character or situation?
- Can you predict some things we might discuss the next time we meet?

The **Illustrator** is a much-coveted role among artistic students. This is a perfect role for the student who rarely completes a written assignment but will draw on a piece of scratch paper all day long. The Illustrator's job is to represent key scenes from the reading. An alternative to drawing scenes might be to create a collage of magazine pictures or to download relevant, appropriate pictures from the Internet. Initially I perceived the role of Illustrator as being somewhat superfluous, until I observed the dialogue that a single picture could generate among students. The Illustrator in one group for *Of Mice and Men* brought in her original drawing of a giant rabbit scolding Lennie just before the climactic scene at the end. I overheard one of her groupmates state, "I didn't get that part of the book before. Now I do."

The **Literary Luminary** brings attention to key lines, quotes, and details from the text. The selections can focus on that which is interesting, powerful, funny, important, puzzling, or worth hearing. As for the personal qualifications of a good Literary Luminary, I tell students that these individuals must be able to read closely and recognize humor, irony, and important ideas. To be truthful, I don't know how to "teach" this role to the students; on the other hand, I have found little need to do much more than model it a few times. Literary Luminaries consistently have strong instincts about what is significant and what is not. In the same *Of Mice and Men* group, I heard the Literary Luminary directing her peers to the following quote in which George tells Lennie, "With us it ain't like that. We got a future. We got somebody to talk to that gives a damn about us. We don't have to sit in no bar room blowing our jack just because we got no place else to go. If them other guys gets in jail, they can rot for all anybody gives a damn. But not us" (Steinbeck, 1993, pp. 13–14).

The **Vocabulary Enricher** looks up definitions for important, unfamiliar words. Though not the most intellectually stimulating role, it is still important, especially for students still gaining competence in English or for students who want to participate but lack the self-confidence to fulfill some of the other roles. Sometimes a group will save this role for a member with inconsistent attendance. A sample entry of a Vocabulary Enricher might look like this:

> Word: disarming
>
> Definition: making it difficult for a person to feel anger or suspicion
>
> Sample Sentence: "Crooks scowled, but Lennie's disarming smile defeated him." (Steinbeck, 1993, p. 69)

Vocabulary Enrichers might then ask others in the group to create their own sentences with the word, or they might consider other forms of the word and how they might be used in sentences.

The **Connector** is a favorite second choice for those students who enjoy being the Discussion Director. The Connector sees relationships between the reading and the real world: students' personal lives, people their age, events at school or in their community or the news. Another possible source of connections can be within the selection itself or between the current reading and literature they have read previously. One Connector related three minor characters from *Of Mice and Men*—Candy, Crooks, and Curley's wife—by pointing out their common experience of being excluded from the group. He asked his classmates to describe times when they too have felt left out and alone.

Students who have artistic ability also enjoy being the **Travel Tracker.** This job is to illustrate scenes and settings from the assigned reading. One Travel Tracker from our discussion of *Of Mice and Men* represented the climactic chapter by drawing two scenes, Lennie in the

barn and the ranch hands playing horseshoes outside. Students identified the contrast between the two simple drawings and how they effectively illustrated the tragedy of Lennie's actions.

Summarizing is a difficult reading skill that must at some point
be taught. The student who elects to be the **Summarizer** for the group
is usually a strong reader and good critical thinker. Good Summarizers
are real assets to their literature circle groups because they help their
peers see the overall picture. A proficient Summarizer is one who can,
for example, extract important details from the first chapter of *Of Mice
and Men*, such as Lennie's simplistic nature, George's frustration at
being Lennie's caretaker, their troubled past, and their mutual devo-
tion. An especially gifted Summarizer might pick up on Steinbeck's
foreshadowing, as well as the undercurrent of impending tragedy.

The **Investigator** has the fascinating assignment of digging up
background information on any topic related to the reading. I like to recommend this role to a student who has trouble staying on topic. It is also
a good role for a student who enjoys finding information on the Internet.
Supplemental information might shed light on geography, history, time
period, music, author, objects, culture, art, or artifacts. The Investigator
for the *Of Mice and Men* group brought in pictures of an early California
ranch and a map of California. His group members were eager to find
where Salinas was located and see how far it was from where they lived.

It is useful to provide a list of these eight roles to groups consisting
of four or five members. Having a choice allows students to find roles
that are best suited to them. The only stipulation I make is that every
group must have a Discussion Director. All the other roles are optional.

Assessing Literature Circles

We walk a fine line when it comes to assessing and evaluating the outcomes of literature circles. If the true intent of this activity is to promote the
making of meaning and a love of reading, then grades and assessment
seem paradoxical. Still, we are under certain professional obligations in
this matter, and for most of us, assigning grades is simply a necessity.

One grade is based on a rubric that assesses each student's participation in his or her group and is based on self-, peer-, and teacher
evaluation. Every member of the group completes an evaluation for all
group members, as does the teacher by circulating from group to
group. After a discussion of the importance of this task, I have found
students' evaluations to be largely honest and accurate. Student and
teacher scores for each student are averaged to determine one grade.
An example of a student's evaluation appears in Figure 7.1.

Name   Ruben   Date   June 6
Title of Book   Joy Luck Club

Please evaluate how well each member of your group functioned during your discussion today.

Student's Name: Linda   Role: Discussion Director

Behavior During Lit Circles	Often	Sometimes	Never
Stayed on task during group activities	X	___	___
Cooperated with other group members	X	___	___
Treated all members with respect	X	___	___
Made significant contribution to the group	X	___	___
Completed assigned work	X	___	___

Comments: <u>She's doing a good job. She's always prepared, and she works hard to try to get everybody to participate in discussion.</u>

I think this student deserves a/an _A_ for today.

Student's Name: Dave   Role: Vocabulary Enricher

Behavior During Lit Circles	Often	Sometimes	Never
Stayed on task during group activities	___	___	X
Cooperated with other group members	___	___	X
Treated all members with respect	___	___	X
Made significant contribution to the group	___	___	X
Completed assigned work	___	___	X

Comments: <u>He was absent again today.</u>

I think this student deserves a/an ___ for today.

Student's Name: Carlos   Role: Illustrator

Behavior During Lit Circles	Often	Sometimes	Never
Stayed on task during group activities	___	X	___
Cooperated with other group members	___	X	___
Treated all members with respect	X	___	___
Made significant contribution to the group	___	X	___
Completed assigned work	X	___	___

Comments: <u>He drew good pictures and we talked about them, but he didn't do much the rest of the time in the group.</u>

I think this student deserves a/an _B–_ for today.

continued on next page

Figure 7.1. Literature Circles: Peer Evaluation

Figure 7.1 continued

Student's Name: Sam   Role: Investigator

Behavior During Lit Circles	Often	Sometimes	Never
Stayed on task during group activities	___	X	___
Cooperated with other group members	___	___	X
Treated all members with respect	___	X	___
Made significant contribution to the group	___	___	X
Completed assigned work	___	___	X

Comments: He didn't bring anything new today, and he didn't really participate in the discussion. I'm not sure he did the reading.

I think this student deserves a/an _C–/D_ for today.

Student's Name: Me (Ruben)   Role: Connector

Behavior During Lit Circles	Often	Sometimes	Never
Stayed on task during group activities	X	___	___
Cooperated with other group members	X	___	___
Treated all members with respect	___	X	___
Made significant contribution to the group	___	X	___
Completed assigned work	X	___	___

Comments: I made some good connections to real life and I participated well in discussion. I was probably too critical of Sam because he didn't do much today.

I think this student deserves a/an _A–_ for today.

Student's Name: _____   Role: _____

Behavior During Lit Circles	Often	Sometimes	Never
Stayed on task during group activities	___	___	___
Cooperated with other group members	___	___	___
Treated all members with respect	___	___	___
Made significant contribution to the group	___	___	___
Completed assigned work	___	___	___

Comments: _____

I think this student deserves a/an _____ for today.

Objective: The purpose of this activity is for your literature circle group to demonstrate your understanding of the book you read. Your finished products will be presented to the class and then placed on display in our school library to encourage other students' interest in reading.

Activity: On a piece of 8 1/2 by 11-inch paper, you will create a publicity brochure for the book you read. Each member of your group will be responsible for providing the text or the graphics for one panel of the brochure.

Instructions:

Fold the sheet of paper lengthwise into three equal parts. The two ends of the paper will fold toward the front (Side A).

Side A (front of paper)

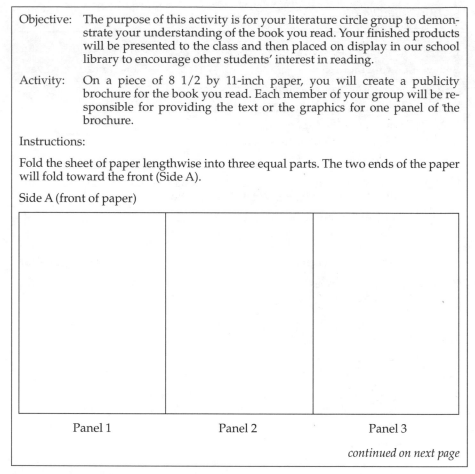

Panel 1   Panel 2   Panel 3

continued on next page

Figure 7.2. Literature Circles Culminating Activity Student Handout: The Publicity Brochure

A second, more substantial grade is usually based on a culminating project or activity. A project I often assign is a compilation of all the individual assignments into one group portfolio that showcases their collected work: the Discussion Director's questions and the group's responses; the Illustrator's drawings; the Vocabulary Enricher's word lists; and so on. These portfolios not only reflect what has occurred in the literature circles, but they also become classroom resources for students making reading selections for future literature circles.

Another assessment activity that has been effective as a culminating activity is to have each group make a three-panel, twofold pub-

Figure 7.2 continued

Side B (back of paper)

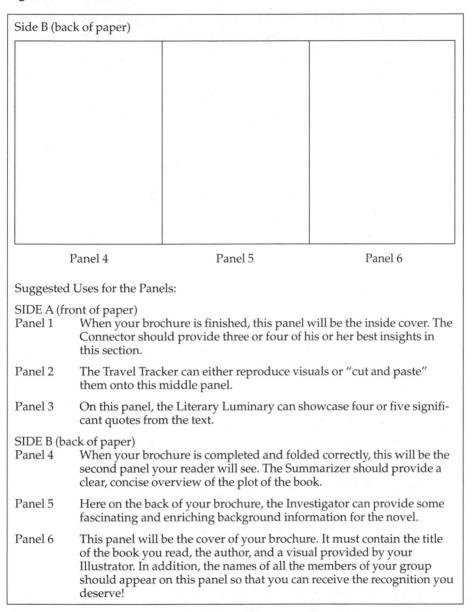

Panel 4   Panel 5   Panel 6

Suggested Uses for the Panels:

SIDE A (front of paper)

Panel 1   When your brochure is finished, this panel will be the inside cover. The Connector should provide three or four of his or her best insights in this section.

Panel 2   The Travel Tracker can either reproduce visuals or "cut and paste" them onto this middle panel.

Panel 3   On this panel, the Literary Luminary can showcase four or five significant quotes from the text.

SIDE B (back of paper)

Panel 4   When your brochure is completed and folded correctly, this will be the second panel your reader will see. The Summarizer should provide a clear, concise overview of the plot of the book.

Panel 5   Here on the back of your brochure, the Investigator can provide some fascinating and enriching background information for the novel.

Panel 6   This panel will be the cover of your brochure. It must contain the title of the book you read, the author, and a visual provided by your Illustrator. In addition, the names of all the members of your group should appear on this panel so that you can receive the recognition you deserve!

licity flier for their book. The information and visuals they use to create the brochure represent the work of all members of the group, as explained in Figure 7.2. Of course, numerous other modifications are possible for the panels.

Making Literature Circles Work

The true intent of literature circles is to allow students to practice and develop the skills and strategies of good readers. Experience has borne out the necessity to directly teach some of these skills. Summarizing, for example, is a skill that requires guidance from me, as does paraphrasing and citing supporting evidence and examples. Similarly, high school students are not comfortable with discord, and multiple, differing viewpoints often result in flaring tempers and rising voices. I have had to teach my students the concept of civilly agreeing to disagree at times. We even practice prefacing statements with phrases such as, "I respect your opinion" or "I can see why you feel that way." All of these skills are perfect topics for ten-minute minilessons that I offer at the start of a class. It is important to remember that even as we empower our students to function with increasing independence, we must not forfeit our responsibility to provide the supports needed for success.

Availability of books for group reading is a problem at many schools. Where I teach, we are currently in the process of allocating some of our budget to the creation of literature circle "reading kits." With so many of us using the literature circle format with our students, we have come up with the idea of creating bins of books—seven titles to a bin, six copies per title—ranging in reading level from easy to difficult. These bins will rotate from classroom to classroom to allow students a constantly changing array of books from which to choose. Here are some of the titles we are considering:

For Less Able Readers

- *A Hero Ain't Nothin' but a Sandwich* (Alice Childress). A thirteen-year-old boy is well on his way to becoming a heroin addict.

- *Hoops* (Walter Dean Myers). Seventeen-year-old Lonnie Jackson hopes that basketball will be his ticket out of Harlem. His coach knows the pressures he will have to face.

- *Number the Stars* (Lois Lowry). This is an inspiring story of a young Danish girl's bravery when Nazis threaten her best friend's safety.

- *Sister of the Bride* (Beverly Cleary). A sixteen-year-old helps her older sister prepare for a wedding.

- *The Slave Dancer* (Paula Fox). Thirteen-year-old Jesse is thrown aboard a slave ship.

- *Taking Sides* (Gary Soto). Lincoln Mendoza moves to a new home, but his friendships and loyalties remain with his friends in his old neighborhood.

- *Then Again, Maybe I Won't* (Judy Blume). Tony's family experiences newly acquired wealth, but Tony has nothing but problems.

For "In the Middle" Readers

- *The Contender* (Robert Lipsyte). Alfred struggles to become a fighter and live respectably in a rundown ghetto.

- *Dragonwings* (Laurence Yep). This story of a Chinese immigrant and his son's attempt to build a flying machine provides a unique perspective of the Chinese American community in the early twentieth century.

- *Gentlehands* (M. E. Kerr). A teenage boy falls in love with an upper-class girl and gets to know his estranged grandfather in a summer that climaxes in a shattering search for Nazi war criminals.

- *Homecoming* (Cynthia Voigt). Four abandoned children, ages six to thirteen, demonstrate courage, resourcefulness, and sheer will to stay together and find a home.

- *It Happened to Nancy* (Anonymous teenager and Beatrice Sparks). A heartbreaking diary recounts a teenager's ordeal after she is date raped at the age of fourteen, contracts AIDS, and dies at sixteen.

- *Nothing but the Truth* (Avi). Ninth grader Philip Malloy decides to annoy his homeroom teacher by humming to "The Star Spangled Banner" and soon finds himself at the center of a national controversy.

- *Stranger with My Face* (Lois Duncan). A seventeen-year-old senses she is being spied on and perhaps impersonated, but then she discovers what is actually occurring.

For Able Readers

- *Buried Onions* (Gary Soto). Nineteen-year-old Eddie drops out of college and struggles to find a place for himself as a Mexican American in Fresno, California.

- *The Hitchhiker's Guide to the Galaxy* (Douglas Adams). Seconds before the Earth is demolished to make way for a galactic freeway, Arthur Dent is plucked off the planet by his friend Ford Prefect, a researcher for the *Hitchhiker's Guide to the Galaxy*.

- *How the Garcia Girls Lost Their Accents* (Julia Alvarez). Four Latinas are uprooted from their pampered life of privilege on an island and thrown into the chaos of life in the big city.

- *Necessary Roughness* (Marie G. Lee). A Korean American teen narrates the story of his family's move from Los Angeles to Minnesota, the racism there, playing high school football, and grieving over the death of his sister.

- *The Road from Home* (David Kherdian). Verna Dumehijan, born to a prosperous Armenian family in Turkey, experiences the end to her happy childhood in 1915 when the Turkish government deports her family.

- *Shizuko's Daughter* (Kyoko Mori). After her mother's suicide, Yuki, living with her distant father and his resentful new wife, must rely on her own inner strength to cope with the tragedy.

- *Someone Is Hiding on Alcatraz Island* (Eve Bunting). Danny has tangled with the toughest gang in school and heads to Alcatraz Island to escape the gang's revenge.

Why Literature Circles Work

Literature circles have become a reliable, successful instructional approach in my classes and in many of my colleagues' classes. I believe that it is the elements of authenticity, empowerment, and collaboration that make them so effective.

As the literacy coordinator for my school of 3,700 students from diverse backgrounds, I have been trying to identify what draws a person to reading—that is, what makes a person become a reader for life. Certainly, our traditional approach to the teaching of literature does not guarantee this conversion from student to lifelong reader. Writing book reports and taking multiple-choice tests at the end of a good novel are not part of an adult's reading experience. In contrast, the behaviors and practices that literature circles encourage are much more authentic. Students are invited to read, think, imagine, question, laugh, and talk. Applebee (1992) exhorts us to "develop programs that emphasize students' ability to develop and defend their interpretations of literary selections, rather than ones that focus only on knowledge about texts, authors, and terminology" (p. 12). When working in literature circles, students respond positively to that which they perceive as genuine and meaningful.

Adolescents are at a developmental stage that directly conflicts with the structure of the traditional classroom. While the traditional

teacher is demanding compliance with seemingly arbitrary expectations, teenagers are seeking to forge their independence and make
their own choices. It is no wonder that so much energy—from teacher
and students alike—can be expended in disciplinary skirmishes. High
school students in particular benefit from opportunities to have a voice
in what they learn, to be given some decision-making power in the
classroom. Literature circles provide these opportunities by allowing
students to select their books and their roles. To some, this might not
seem a tremendous amount of choice, but it is one step closer to making the classroom better suited to the psychosocial needs of adolescents. Moreover, the literature circle format validates the opinions and
perspectives of our students, something that does not happen enough
in the high school classroom. According to Langer (1992), "Schooling
rarely asks students to share their own understandings of a text, nor
does it help students learn to build richer ones through the exploration
of possibilities" (p. 38). It has been my experience that the lively dis-
course and exchange of diverse perspectives in literature circles have
done more to promote critical reading in my students than most of the
other learning situations I have facilitated.

The virtues of cooperative learning have been extolled for years,
but too often in practice we set up students for failure. We throw them
into groups and give them complex tasks that require them to know
how to speak, listen, negotiate, delegate, initiate, and compromise.
And we have assumed that they have the skills to do all of these things
successfully! Then, when small-group activities are not successful,
teachers abandon group work altogether. As a result, students rarely
experience the true power and potential of collaboration. Literature
circles avoid those fatal assumptions. They provide a safe and support-
ive structure within which our students can interact. They define the
roles that our students are asked to assume and allow them the time to
develop important interpersonal communication skills. Best of all, they
inevitably provide our students with proof that they will benefit from
the respectful sharing and receiving of each person's unique talents
and insights.

It has been a great source of joy to see my students grow in their
reading abilities as a result of their experiences in literature circles.
When we put students in the center of their own learning process, provide them with support and encouragement, and trust in their ability
to rise to our expectations, we can step back and watch true learning in
action.

References

Applebee, A. N. (1992). The background of reform. In J. A. Langer (Ed.), *Literature instruction: A focus on student response* (pp. 1–18). Urbana, IL: National Council of Teachers of English.

Brooks, J. G., & Brooks, M. G. (1993). *In search of understanding: The case for constructivist classrooms*. Alexandria, VA: Association for Supervision and Curriculum Development.

Daniels, H. (1994). *Literature circles: Voice and choice in the student-centered classroom*. York, ME: Stenhouse.

Langer, J. A. (1992). Rethinking literature instruction. In J. A. Langer (Ed.), *Literature instruction: A focus on student response* (pp. 35–53). Urbana, IL: National Council of Teachers of English.

LiteratureCircles.com. (2000). Available: http://www.literaturecircles.com/.

Steinbeck, J. (1993). *Of mice and men*. New York: Penguin Books. (Originally published 1937).

8 By Any Other Name: Reconnecting Readers in the High School

Teri S. Lesesne
Sam Houston State University

Lois Buckman
Moorhead Junior/Caney Creek Senior High
Academic Complex, Texas

They are known by many names: reluctant readers, aliterate students, unmotivated learners. But as the wise old bard wrote centuries ago, "A rose by any other name . . . ." No matter what label we apply, these students are in *your* classroom. What happened to these students who all began their academic careers with the same fervent wish that first day of kindergarten: that they learn to read independently? What caused these eager beavers to transform into meager readers? More important, what can we do to reignite that early passion to read? These questions are the focus of a long-term study we have conducted with reluctant readers. Our purpose in this chapter is twofold: First, we discuss reasons why we lose readers over the course of their academic journey. Then, we offer some suggestions for reconnecting these students to the pleasures of reading.

Before we begin our journey, however, we wish to answer one essential question: Why are we so concerned about students reading for pleasure? Jim Trelease, in his *Read-Aloud Handbook* (1995), suggests that we do a good job in our schools of creating school-time readers. Where many schools fail is in creating lifetime readers. What are lifetime readers? Here is a quick quiz. How many of you have books on your bedside table (or under the bed), in your bathroom, in the backseats of your cars? Any of you who raised your hands—you are lifetime readers. You read not because it is required, but because you desire to read. As a matter of fact, we already knew you were lifetime readers: you are reading this book! Why is it so important to create lifetime readers? Trelease goes on to report that 75 percent of high school seniors report they will never voluntarily read once they graduate. So, apart from making you incredibly sad, what other more compelling reasons are there for us to create more lifetime readers? Many of us plan to retire from the profession at some point. Our leaders of the future are the kids we graduate now.

Where many schools fail is in creating lifetime readers.

If these future leaders are not readers, where do they obtain information? From other, nonprint media. Think about that for a moment. Chilling enough? But also consider this: if we can convince students that reading is a pleasurable activity, they are more likely to read and to read with a positive attitude. And the more they read, and enjoy their reading, the better their reading fluency and reading skills. With stronger capabilities, they will read more and continue to build fluency and skills. It's a circular pattern and one we teachers want to perpetuate at the high school level.

Losing Readers

Children arrive the first day of kindergarten full of expectations. They speed through those early elementary years acquiring the skills and abilities and qualities they will need for a lifetime of learning. And somewhere along the way, reluctant readers begin to lose their interest in reading for pleasure. What happens to make these students disconnect? As teachers we asked that question of ourselves many times. A few years ago, we decided that perhaps the best answers would come from the students themselves. That decision led us to put together a research project that would attempt to recover lost readers and reintroduce the idea of reading as a pleasurable activity. The first step in our project was to survey students in an attempt to understand why reading was no longer a priority in their lives and what we could do to pull students back to books. The first thing we discovered was that these students were not at all reluctant to tell us why they were less than enthusiastic readers. They identified three factors that negatively affected their reading habits and attitudes. We have categorized these factors as book, teacher, and classroom qualities. We add another factor to our discussion: reader variables.

Push, Push, Push . . .

The chief complaint we heard from the students we surveyed was that teachers did not seem to know any good books for them to read. "What teachers are always trying to do to me," insisted one young woman, "is to force me to read books *she* likes. I don't like the same kind of books she does, but when I tell her that, she tells me these books are good for me. Who cares if they are *good* for me? I want books that are just plain *good*." Another student added, "If a teacher really wanted to encourage me to read more, she should talk to me about what I'd like to see in a book. Teachers should know more about what I might want to read instead of always thinking they know better than me about what makes a good book." Survey after survey noted similar comments. Students wanted teachers to acknowledge the reading they were doing already. Instead, most felt that teachers did not understand what makes for a good book.

So we pressed forward with more questions: What qualities attract you to a book? Where do you get recommendations for books? What should a teacher do to make you want to read more? Again, we found students anxious to share their thoughts and feelings. Figure 8.1 presents the items on the student survey that addressed the qualities of a book that might attract readers.

Students' responses make it readily apparent that many make decisions about books based on qualities that have little or nothing to do with the book itself but with what we might characterize as marketing qualities. The majority of students we surveyed indicated that they select books based on their covers (28 percent).

At a recent American Library Association conference, publishers' representatives spoke about this phenomenon, agreeing that cover art is essential for capturing the attention of the teen market, whether these teens are in school, or in a bookstore, or shopping for books online. Examination of cover art, therefore, might make for an interesting practice in the classroom. Take, for example, a young adult book that has been in print long enough to have gone through many editions. *The Outsiders* by S. E. Hinton (1967) is one such book. Since its initial publication, the book has undergone many face-lifts. Original cover art was dramatic and abstract, with shadowy figures in black set against a vibrant red background. A later edition of the same novel featured photographs of some of the "Brat Pack" stars who were featured in the movie version of the novel, including Patrick Swayze and Tom Cruise. The most recent cover celebrates the thirtieth anniversary of this classic work of adolescent literature. It too is distinctive.

QUALITY	PERCENT OF RESPONSES
Thickness of the book (length)	18%
Cover art	28%
Subject of the book	5%
Title of the book	13%
Paperback format	15%
Book flap summary	11%
First chapter	5%
Other	2%

Figure 8.1. Students' Responses to the Question, "What qualities do you look for when selecting a book?"

If, then, students focus on the cover art of a book, use this factor as the basis for a classroom lesson. Students could first discuss the cover of the book in terms of what it leads them to surmise about its contents prior to reading. Another approach would be to have students survey others in the school about the types of book covers they find enticing and/or boring and report their findings to the class with some analysis of the results (a miniresearch paper, if you will). Students might also be encouraged to design their own covers for books. Look at how many skills are involved in what seems to be a simple assignment. Students must be able to do the following:

- summarize the novel for the book flap
- locate and summarize information about the author for the back flap
- decide whether the cover is to be an abstract or more concrete representation of the contents
- either locate printed reviews for the back cover or interview others for quotes

Of course, if your friendly school librarian is smart, he or she will laminate these student-designed covers and use them for a display that is sure to stop those who drift aimlessly through the library in search of good books to read.

Other than the cover, students turn a critical eye to the thickness (or perhaps thinness is more accurate) of their selections. Length remains a consideration for readers of all ages and abilities. Let's face it; if we are given the choice between a thick volume and a thin one, most of us would opt for the latter as well. What we need to do, then, is locate some good books that present a thin profile to our students. Joni Bodart's *100 World-Class Thin Books, or, What to Read When Your Book Report Is Due Tomorrow* (1993) is a handy resource here. Bodart reminds us that many quality pieces of literature are also relatively short. Take, for instance, John Steinbeck's *Of Mice and Men* (1937), at 128 pages in length, or perhaps *A Day No Pigs Would Die* by Robert Newton Peck (1972), only 150 pages long. Not only does Bodart provide titles of the books, but each entry also contains an annotation to give readers an indication of the book's contents. Discussion questions, key concepts and themes, and even ideas for book report activities are provided for each selection in this wonderful book, which should be a part of your professional library and made available to the intended audience—your students.

What Can *We* Do?

One of our closest friends and colleagues admitted to us recently that when he hears the word *poetry* he smells formaldehyde. What he (and many others, we are willing to wager) remembers about the study of poetry in the classroom is that it was suspiciously similar to the dissections occurring in biology lab. The students we surveyed agreed with the assessment of this former English teacher. "Teachers always seem to do the same things with books year after year," said one tenth grader. "Do all of you guys get together and decide exactly what you are going to say and do?" queried another sophomore.

All right, we responded, what advice would you give a teacher who wants to encourage you to read more? Once again we discovered that students have some definite ideas about the qualities they would find motivational in teachers and in their classrooms. After gathering responses from these students, we assembled a list of ten qualities they found motivational in teachers and classrooms. We then used that list as part of our survey of other students in the school to determine whether these same qualities were important to others. Students were asked to check any and all of the items they found to be motivational. Figure 8.2 presents the responses of the larger group.

The factors of interest, choice, and time appear on survey after survey. Students want teachers who care about what students want to read, who ask for book suggestions, and who read books recommended by students. "If teachers show interest in the books their students are already reading on their own," one student reasoned, "I would probably be more willing to read books they suggest later. You

QUALITY	PERCENT OF RESPONSES
Teachers who read aloud daily	80%
Classroom libraries	75%
Teachers who allow selection in reading material	90%
Teachers who ask me what I like to read	100%
Teachers who read the books I recommend	65%
Teachers who are "caught" reading	55%
Teachers who have us talk about books in class	45%
Places to curl up with books in class	55%
Time to read at school	80%
Listening to books on tape	55%

Figure 8.2. Qualities of Motivational Teachers and Classrooms

need to start with where I am right now instead of where you would like me to be." Terry Ley (1979) allowed his students some choice in reading material in what he called directed independent reading (DIR). DIR allows students to select reading material. Moreover, it guarantees that teachers will schedule valuable class time for independent reading and provide choices for follow-up activities. We have discovered during the course of our five-year study of at-risk students that if we involve students in book selection, they are much more likely to read the books. We have removed books from the study because one group of students did not care for the titles. Conversely, we have added books students have recommended for inclusion. Of course, we are also aware that what interests one group of students might not interest another group of students in the same school in the same grade. Isn't that part of what makes teaching an inexact science? Students are individuals with individual tastes and interests. Yet sometimes publishers treat them as one entity, offering them only one bill of fare. Students want the opportunity to find books they like and to share them with their teachers.

Students want the chance to self-select some of their books and not always be tied to a restrictive list. One young man put it succinctly: "Let me pick a book from, say, five or six titles. Let me have some choice in what we will read in class sometimes." Notice that this student is requesting choice but not insisting that the choice be totally open. Instead, he is suggesting what we hear from students time and again in our research: let us have some limited selection. Lois knows the value of this factor firsthand as a high school librarian. Week after week she watches as students pour through the doors of the library. Many are on a quest—to find that perfect good book to read. Once they are confronted with 25,000 plus possibilities, however, their eyes glaze over. How is it possible to find the perfect book among such an overwhelming collection? Lois's task, and that of the English teachers who bring students to the library, is to provide some guidance, to find out what kids are searching for, and to provide them with several books from which to select.

Through our research study, we wanted to find a way to make sure that every time our students came to the library in search of a good book to read, they would have a particular place set aside where they could browse and make their selection. We had heard our friend Kylene Beers discuss her Good Book Box and decided to use a variation, the Good Book Cart. Through a grant from the ALAN Foundation (see the Some Concrete Book and Resource Suggestions section), we purchased multiple copies of ten works of YA literature. Lois placed these on a library book cart and did two important things. First, she wheeled the cart to individual classrooms (if the mountain won't come to Mohammed . . .). There in the classroom she gave students an introduction to each of the books through a technique called book talking (more about this in the Book Talk subsection). Students were informed that the cart would be placed in Lois's office and that they could come by any time to select books from the cart. We watched for reactions to this idea. Over the course of the first few weeks, students came by one at a time to browse the cart. Occasionally they asked questions about a particular book. They then checked out the book, making sure it got placed back on the cart when they returned it. Eventually, the scene changed a bit; students began to drag friends along for their book browsing, assuring them that they knew where the "good books" were being kept. In this way, students were allowed choice in their reading fare, and teachers reported that their students were reading more on their own.

Finally, students surveyed asked for more time at school for reading, as well as for a comfortable place to read. These two requests make a lot of sense. We know that once students leave school for the day, many have commitments that cut short the time they have to read at home. Many of our students are involved in extracurricular activities such as sports and music. Many more have responsibilities at home or have part-time jobs. And then, of course, there is the fact that most have televisions, VCRs, computers, and video games at home. We can choose to fight against these factors that rob our students of the time they have to read outside of school, or we can simply provide additional time *in* school for reading. Making the classroom environment comfortable for reading is also important to students. How many of us read at home sitting upright at a desk? One of Teri's favorite places to read is curled up on the couch. Lois reads nightly in bed. We need to allow students some freedom of movement in the classroom for extended silent reading, providing pillows, bean bags, and other items that make the classroom more like the students' home environments.

We have seen so far that teacher, book, and classroom factors play essential roles in students' reading interests and habits. What about those variables over which we have no control? Three additional factors play some role in this process: age, gender, and ability. Of these three factors, the gender of the reader seems to be the most important in our study of reluctant readers. We have seen no significant differences in responses based on age or reading ability. But the old adage, "Boys want to read about boys and girls want to read about girls," holds true for the students we surveyed. Boys prefer a story in which the main character is male; girls want to read stories with female main characters.

This gender difference poses a problem and challenges the age-old "one size fits all" curriculum, in which all students read the same literary work at the same pace and are evaluated in the same manner. Our research suggests that providing students some choice motivates them to read more. So as we add titles to our Good Book Cart, we try to keep a balance between books that will appeal to girls and those that will appeal mainly to boys. There is some crossover, of course, but it is as rare to find a boy reading romance as to find a girl delving into high fantasy. Keeping in mind this difference is essential.

Reconnecting Readers

So, what can we do to reconnect these aliterate students in our classrooms? We offer two simple suggestions that can be implemented easily in any classroom.

Book Talks

In addition to placing our "special" books on a Good Book Cart, Lois also takes the time to give students personal introductions to the books through book talking. The purpose of book talking is to give students some idea of the contents of the books from which they will make their selections. An ideal book talk should whet readers' appetites—an appetizer, if you will, before the consumption of the entire story. Figure 8.3 provides some suggestions for planning and giving book talks. Scholastic Press online (www.scholastic.com) offers examples of book talks by

---

DO talk about books that you have read.
This is the first rule and one never to be broken. If you have not previewed the material, you cannot be certain it is appropriate for your students.

DO combine telling a bit of the story with a brief read-aloud.
Selecting a passage that is humorous or suspenseful works well.

DO have the books available for students to check out.
Seize the moment and allow students to take the books immediately. Making them wait may mean a loss of interest.

DO combine a variety of genres, including nonfiction.
Remember that the interests and preferences of your audience are diverse.
Be sure to include books in a variety of styles and genres.

DON'T tell the whole story.
If we tell students too much of a story, there is little incentive for them to check out the book and read on their own.

DON'T talk about books you did not like.
You simply cannot fake it for the students. It is possible, however, to have someone else book talk along with you to ensure that a variety of books is presented. So, if you loathe fantasy, find a colleague who is an aficionado and enlist his or her assistance.

Figure 8.3. Suggestions for Book Talks

Joni Bodart, one of the leading figures in this art of motivating readers. But we suggest tailoring book talks to your individual personality. Canned book talks seldom work for others as well as for the person who originated them.

Mentoring

For the past several years, we have paired students from the public schools with preservice teachers enrolled in a YA literature class at Sam Houston State University in a unique mentoring program called STOMP. The Student Teacher On-Line Mentoring Project provides at-risk secondary students with mentors who plan to teach adolescents after graduation. Early each semester, the two groups of students meet in person at Lois's school. They interview one another and make a decision about one or more books they will read in common over the next fifteen weeks. Site visits occur monthly, but students keep in touch between visits through e-mail.

This one-to-one mentoring has paid off over the years. We have seen students who were totally disengaged become active members of the Reading Club. Because Lois's school houses grades 7–12, we have been able to observe these students even after they leave the program at the end of the fifteen weeks. The results of this mentoring project have been gratifying: not one student involved in the project has dropped out of school; all have graduated (and some are the first in their families to achieve this). These students are scoring passing grades on the state-mandated assessments as well, something that pleases school district administrators, teachers, and parents. Years after participation several students are keeping in touch, corresponding about books and reading. Mentoring takes very little time from other classroom activities. Indeed, some students come to Lois's library before school begins simply to send e-mail to their university mentor. The relative ease of access to the Internet makes mentoring possible even when schools are far away from the nearest university. This project is one that can, and should, be readily replicated in other schools.

Some Concrete Book and Resource Suggestions

One of the questions teachers ask most frequently is how to select materials to use with these at-risk high school students. How can we remain accountable to the curriculum while balancing the needs of the individual students in our classrooms? We know from experience and from our research that the traditional canon is not often effective in motivating these students to read. We are also aware, however, that some curricular requirements are nonnegotiable. We suggest using the YA titles discussed in the following paragraphs as a bridge to the classics.

Many English classes start off the year with a short story unit found in the literature anthology. This is a good way to hook the students because the readings are short; unfortunately, the stories are not always appealing to these readers. To help grab and maintain the students' attention, you might want to mix in works from new short story collections that speak to adolescent readers. One possibility is *Doing Time: Notes from the Undergrad* by Rob Thomas (1997). The premise of this collection is that in order to graduate from high school, each student is required to do two hundred hours of community service. Each student must then submit a written report on his or her activities. These "reports" form the short stories that make up *Doing Time*. Jill volunteers at Lifeline, a help line for teenagers. A key element of her job is privacy. When the phone rings and an anonymous voice wants to know the options for an unplanned pregnancy, Jill recognizes the voice. She tells only one person, but soon everyone knows. Another student, Laura, volunteers in a convalescent home where she meets the boy of her dreams. The only problem is that he has sustained brain damage from an accident. There are ten students, ten stories; each is separate and distinct and can be read on its own. The characters are tied together through their shared community service, which makes this collection read almost like a novel.

Whitechurch by Chris Lynch (1999) is another story collection connected by the characters, in this case three good friends: Pauly, Lilly, and Oakley. Their stories are so tightly woven that they resemble a novel, with pieces that are an integral part of the whole. Pauly and Oakley are extremely close friends until Lilly moves to town. Immediately, a three-way friendship blossoms. Eventually, Lilly begins to date Pauly, even though his behavior becomes more volatile. Lilly seems unaware that Oakley is in love with her. In the summer after they graduate from high school, Pauly becomes obsessed with preventing Lilly from going away to college. It is a dangerous obsession, one that ultimately changes the lives of all three characters. When you ask students to respond to the readings, the concept of interconnected stories can be fruitful. They could analyze how the stories work together as a unit and yet still stand alone.

As often as not, reading drama in a high school English class means reading Shakespeare. Despite the fact that recent movies have helped to make Shakespeare more of a real person and his work more accessible to students, the archaic language is often a stumbling block for readers. *Monster,* a story that unfolds as a movie script, will excite the most reluctant reader and help prepare students for more difficult works later. Author Walter Dean Myers (1999) weaves together the script and the journal entries written by Steve Harmon, who is on trial for his role in a fatal shooting during a robbery. The prosecutor contends that Steve acted as the lookout and therefore shares equal responsibility for the killing. Steve's guilt isn't what drives the plot; rather, the story focuses on Steve's anguish throughout the day-by-day events of the courtroom. *Monster* works in the classroom on several levels. The plot jumps off the page so little needs to be done to motivate reading. The story has no definitive conclusion. Myers does not tell the reader if Steve was really innocent, allowing students the opportunity to debate guilt and innocence. The mixed formats of drama and journal writing can also lead to some interesting writing assignments. Steve's voice is so strong as he languishes in his jail cell at night that this book presents a perfect opportunity for discussing the impact of voice in a literary work.

Nonfiction is an appealing genre for high school students; it is also one of the most ignored. *Boys Will Be* by Bruce Brooks (1995) is a series of essays that could readily be assigned along with other, more traditional essays. Brooks's topics range from hero worship in sports to interpersonal relationships. "Ten Things You Cannot Expect Your Mom to Come Close to Understanding" is as hilarious as it is true. What to do about bullies and "Eight Reasons Why Ice Hockey Kicks Football's Tutu" are right on the mark. Young men who won't read anything will find that this book speaks to them.

Teachers are always looking for good multicultural literature, and one such book is *Parrot in the Oven: Mi Vida* by Victor Martinez (1998). Told in a series of vignettes, this novel is appropriate for whole-class reading. Manuel lives with his mother, his alcoholic father, and an older brother who drifts from job to job. His father equates people with money and says that Manuel is like a penny, not worth much. Manuel longs for respect, but how to find it is a big question in his life. Will he gain respect if he joins a gang, or will respect be earned through boxing? Manuel is not happy with his life, and in this coming-of-age novel he searches for answers to issues many adolescents face.

When poetry is mentioned, many students inwardly—or outwardly—cringe. To breathe excitement into the genre, we must look to some of the exciting new anthologies. Students will enjoy poetry when they are introduced to *I Feel a Little Jumpy around You*, edited by Naomi Sahib Nye and Paul B. Janeczko (1996). This collection has wide appeal and features poems on similar subjects set side by side. One poem is written by a woman, the other by a man. The poems address the same topic, and readers can immediately see the different perspectives.

How do we decide which books to use with our students? Of course, we allow students to give us some direction; we also read everything we can and use professional judgment about which books to include. But it is impossible to read everything that is available. For further help, we turn to YALSA, a section of the American Library Association. This group annually publishes the Best Books for Young Adults list, a wonderful selection tool. This list and others they generate for senior high (and middle) schools can be found at http://www.ala.org/yalsa/booklists/index.html.

TAYSHAS is a list generated for high school students by a committee of the Texas Library Association. A committee of secondary librarians reads recommended books and votes on which to include on the list. This high school Web site can be found at http://www.txla.org/groups/yart/TAYSHASLISTS.html.

Books for You: An Annotated Booklist for Senior High (Beers & Lesesne, 2001) is a publication of the National Council of Teachers of English that includes an extensive listing of annotated book entries arranged thematically. For further information, visit NCTE at http://www.ncte.org.

ALAN, the Assembly on Literature for Adolescents of the National Council of Teachers of English, is a valuable organization for high school teachers. *The ALAN Review*, published three times a year, contains articles written by YA authors as well as a clip-and-file review section of the most recent YA literature. You can also visit this site on the Internet at http://www.scholar.lib.vt.edu/ejournals/ALAN/alan-review.html.

Where from Here?

The projects and activities described in this chapter grew out of the need to reconnect adolescent readers to reading. Not in many years has there been such a wonderful array of literature available to adolescents. Numerous appealing and appropriate works are published each year for the high school student, certainly a development we should cheer. We English teachers need to take advantage of this treasure trove and use it to lure students back to their early love of books and reading.

References

Beers, K., & Lesesne, T. S. (Eds.). (2001). *Books for you: An annotated booklist for senior high* (14th ed.). Urbana, IL: National Council of Teachers of English.

Bodart, J. (1993). *100 world-class thin books, or, What to read when your book report is due tomorrow*. Englewood, CO: Libraries Unlimited.

Brooks, B. (1995). *Boys will be*. New York: Hyperion.

Hinton, S. E. (1967). *The outsiders*. New York: Viking Press.

Ley, T. C. (1979). Getting kids into books: The importance of individualized reading. *Media and Methods, 15*(7), 21–24.

Lynch, C. (1999). *Whitechurch*. New York: HarperCollins.

Martinez, V. (1998). *Parrot in the oven: Mi vida*. New York: Harper Trophy.

Myers, W. D. (1999). *Monster*. New York: HarperCollins.

Nye, N. S., & Janeczko, P. (1996). *I feel a little jumpy around you: A book of her poems and his poems collected in Paris*. New York: Simon & Schuster.

Peck, R. N. (1972). *A day no pigs would die*. New York: Knopf.

Steinbeck, J. (1937). *Of mice and men*. New York: Modern Library.

Thomas, R. (1997). *Doing time: Notes from the undergrad*. New York: Simon & Schuster.

Trelease, J. (1995). *The read-aloud handbook* (4th ed.). New York: Penguin Books.

9 The Place of Young Adult Literature in Secondary Reading Programs

Lois T. Stover
St. Mary's College of Maryland

Two Readers—One Problem

I recently received a letter from a former student who was spending her summer tutoring high school students in reading. Nancy wrote,

> Richie called me at 10:00 last night. He didn't even say his name. He just blurted out, "Jeff's dying!" Richie is reading Crutcher's *Stotan!* and he's so involved with the book that he wanted to talk about it right then, right away. It was so cool! When I pointed out to him that he was not only reading, but was engaging with a book—something he'd said he'd never done—he commented that the books he was given in school just weren't worth his time, but that Crutcher's book is "cool because it's about real kids and they have problems I have with girls and parents and they're in sports with their friends so they're sort of like me." The characters and their relationships pulled him into the book and *made* him want to read.

Nancy's letter reminded me of another letter I received several years ago, this one from a high school friend. This woman went to an Ivy League school, double-majored in French and political science, achieved Phi Beta Kappa status, and then attended law school. After becoming a partner in her law firm, she and her husband started a family, and at the time of this particular letter, she was a mother to two young girls who were learning to read. My friend commented that now, in her midthirties, after a great deal of academic and professional success, she was finally reading for pleasure again. She noted that reading with her daughters, relearning from them the delights of getting lost in a text, of becoming part of a fictional world, reminded her that through reading, she could escape from the demands of everyday life, learn about others, go back—or forward—in time, and in general just relax.

My friend also noted that our high school senior English course, during which we'd had to read at least a book a week, take notes, and write a critical paper of some sort, had been part of the reason she had not read for pleasure in such a long time. This highly competent and able reader had been turned off to the literary experience by her teacher's choice of texts and related demands; my friend wrote that while she had been able to analyze important texts, from Hardy's *Tess of the D'Urbervilles* to Faulkner's *As I Lay Dying*, she had felt no real connection with the characters and so had come to see reading as an academic task, something that might engage her head but not her heart. Years later, as her daughters showed their excitement about reading, she was reminded of herself as a reader prior to beginning high school English.

Obviously, some students who become passionate about reading as children maintain their enthusiasm throughout middle and high school, and even choose to major in English as a way to further immerse themselves in literary worlds. It is also true that a variety of factors in contemporary society affect whether students become readers. Given that young adults are surrounded by video games and large-screen televisions and have easy access to movie theaters and video stores, books face a great deal of competition for time in the adolescent's daily schedule. Our young people often come of age in homes in which reading is not a valued activity, and the demands of athletics, part-time jobs, and school work also take up time that might otherwise be available for reading. Teachers have little control over these elements of students' lives.

But both Richie and my old high school friend, one a reluctant reader in need of remedial support to improve his skills and the other a sophisticated and "successful" reader, demonstrate one failure of the reading program over which teachers *do* have some control. Each indicates that his or her antipathy for reading developed as a result of feeling unconnected to the books they were assigned. In one case, the resulting lack of enthusiasm contributed to a lack of progress in developing skill as a reader; in the other, it led the individual to stop reading on her own. Both readers are examples of a common problem within traditional high school reading and English programs: Students often fail to develop as lifelong readers, and thus they fail to meet one of the primary goals of the reading program. Indeed, Bushman and Bushman (1997) find that surveys of adults who identify themselves as readers indicate that these adults became readers *in spite of, rather than because of,* their reading experiences in high school (p. 3).

Paradoxically, the literature so often presented to young adult readers today as the stuff of essays and classroom literary analysis was, when originally published, gobbled up by hungry young adult readers of the times. Hunter, in *Before Novels* (1990), notes that during the second half of the seventeenth century, when England experienced a sharp rise in literacy levels, it was the young who had the "skill, as well as the motivation" (p. 80), to read. He suggests,

> Novels have traditionally captured a disproportionate readership among the young, perhaps because youth seek knowledge the novel contains, perhaps because new readers are perpetually seeking promising new outlets as alternatives to what their elders recommend. . . . *Literary critics habitually, in their pursuit of artistic and aesthetic concerns, tend to underrate the "real-life" issues that draw readers to novels or condition their choices of reading material more generally—questions about how the world works and how other people make the structural decisions that face us all.* (p. 79, emphasis added)

Those few books that stand out in surveys of young adult readers as eliciting enthusiastic responses confirm a similar hunger. For several years, Robin Bates, a colleague of mine in our English department, has been asking his students to complete papers chronicling their reading histories. In these papers, students identify the most significant stories in their lives, and Salinger's *Catcher in the Rye* (1951) is the title most frequently mentioned. Other assigned works from their high school English courses that students cite include *A Separate Peace* (1960) by Knowles and Golding's *Lord of the Flies* (1955) (Bates, 1995).

All of these stories are about adolescent protagonists with whom young readers feel a kinship. Like Richie, the student needing remedial help who may never take a college class, the students in Bates's courses report responding dramatically to such books because they allow, or even force, their readers to rethink their views of themselves. Says one young woman about her reaction to the Knowles and Golding books,

> I was even more horrified by the fact that the actions seemed to stem from an intense jealousy. . . . [T]he reason that this horrified me is that I also am prone to attacks of intense jealousy, especially of my best friends. I wondered whether I might do something so reprehensible one day, not thinking, compelled by my subconscious. (Seymour, 1990, p. 4)

If such engagement were the norm in our high school classrooms, all would be well. The sad fact of the matter is, however, that many of our students share the experiences of either Richie or my high school friend. While it can be argued that a good teacher should be able to help students feel points of connection between their own lives and "classic" texts, the New Critical approach still favored in high school reading and literature classes often leads teen readers to view reading as an academic task, rather than as a way of learning more about themselves, others, and the world. The result, as Bushman and Bushman (1997) state, is that the students only learn *about* literature; they do not engage with it:

> If schools and teachers want students to understand what they read, to interact with the literature so that they can make connections to their own lives, to make critical judgments that will enhance their intellectual, emotional, and moral development, and perhaps most importantly, to become lifelong readers, schools and teachers must evaluate the literature curriculum and make the necessary changes so that students can, indeed, achieve success in these areas. (p. 3)

One possible strategy for making the literature curriculum more engaging is to weave young adult literature throughout the curriculum in a variety of ways. I believe that doing so will allow teachers to better meet Bushman and Bushman's (1997) program goals while also meeting the needs of students like Richie and my lawyer friend. Young adult literature is, by definition, about the problems and issues of adolescence; therefore, such literature can motivate many adolescent readers more readily than those works so often presented in surveys of British, American, and world literature. Furthermore, if it is taught well, YA literature can serve those curricular goals related to development of an informed and critical lifelong reader, as well as bridge the gap into literary classics that may seem, on the surface, to be emotionally distanced from the high school reader.

A Definition of YA Literature

Research by Bates (1995), Bushman and Bushman (1997), and others indicates at least one important reason why students such as Richie often fail to be drawn into reading. Adolescents demand strategies for living from their reading and can be turned off to reading if they are not provided with books that meet this demand. The literature presented to them in reading and/or English programs frequently does not speak to this need to look into a mirror and discover answers to the eternal "Who am I?" question of adolescence.

On the other hand, Brown and Stephens (1995), writing on *Teaching Young Adult Literature,* define this genre by stating that it does meet this need:

> In simple terms, young adult literature may be defined as books written specifically for and about youth. It is a body of literature written for an adolescent audience that is, in turn, about the lives, experiences, aspirations, and problems of young people. In other words, the term "young adult literature" describes the primary audience for these works as well as the subject matter they explore. (p. 6)

Young adults are both the subject matter of and the audience for books—both fiction and nonfiction—marketed by publishers as YA literature. Thematically, at their core such works almost always deal with questions of identity. In *Stotan!* (1986), which chronicles the senior year, particularly the swim-meet season, of the protagonist Walker, Crutcher shows this young man struggling to determine his own strengths, how to define manhood, and where his future might take him. Richie responded to Walker and his friends because he too was dealing with these kinds of questions.

> *Young adults are both the subject matter of and the audience for books—both fiction and nonfiction— marketed by publishers as YA literature. Thematically, at their core such works almost always deal with questions of identity.*

These works also share several other common characteristics. Most YA literature has one main character, a young adult anywhere from twelve to twenty years old. For instance, in Crutcher's *Stotan!* readers are introduced to the other members of Walker's swim team through his perspective. One major plot, with few subplots, occurs within a relatively short time span. Again, as an example, in *Stotan!* the action takes place primarily during one grueling week of physical and emotional endurance tests prior to the beginning of the swim season. Authors of YA books generally create only one major setting, and the typical length of a YA novel is 125 to 220 pages. Writers of these books conventionally use language—vocabulary, syntax, structure—that echoes the language of young adults themselves.

Nevertheless, good YA literature is not simplistic. It deals with themes and issues that mirror the concerns of the society out of which it is produced; it does so in ways that help readers understand the complexities and shades of gray involved in dealing with these issues. Once more, for instance, in *Stotan!*, Crutcher's characters deal with child abuse, family relationships and battered wives, leukemia, and sexuality. Nuclear holocaust, environmental devastation, power and political issues, racial prejudice, homophobia, and death, as well as topics such as first relationships, body image, struggles with parents, or part-time jobs, can all be found in YA books. These issues are of importance to young adults as well as significant in our ever-changing world.

It is important to remember that the nature of young adults makes it difficult to be too precise about the characteristics of their reading. In *Literature for Today's Young Adults,* Donelson and Nilsen (2001) go so far as to define young adult literature as "anything that readers between the approximate ages of twelve and twenty choose to read (as opposed to what they may be coerced to read for class assignments)" (p. 6). As adolescents struggle toward identity—dealing with their own changing bodies, changing roles within family and society, and changing relationships—their reading tastes and habits change. Furthermore, the good writers for this audience, like all good artists, quite frequently test the boundaries of the genre. Therefore, books published as "young adult," such as Rinaldi's historical fiction, may run over three hundred pages in paperback and still find readers. Rodowsky's *Julie's Daughter* (1985) has multiple narrators who speak in alternating chapters, rather than the typical single narrator. Draper's *Tears of a Tiger* (1994) is structurally complex, using poetry, newspaper articles, dialogue, and other forms of writing to tell the tale of how one young man copes with the death of his friend, and Bruchac's *Sacajawea* (2000) combines alternating points of view, fictional diary entries, and passages from historical Lewis and Clark documents; yet both books have a strong adolescent readership. In general, however, YA literature uses protagonists and content that appeal to its specific audience, and it is crafted to be accessible to readers still developing their abilities to interact with texts of various sorts.

As an aside, some adolescents do not like the term *young adult literature,* feeling that it is somewhat demeaning. Regardless of what teachers call such texts, the point is that they should use them.

The Value of Including YA Literature in Secondary Reading Programs

I would like to make it clear that I do not want to eliminate from reading programs those classic works of literature that often serve as an introduction to the history of American, British, and world literatures. Good teachers *can* find ways to engage more sophisticated readers with these texts. Also, I am not saying that students should not have to work hard as readers. What I propose is that teachers enrich their reading programs by providing students with quality YA literature for two major reasons. First, YA literature is developmentally appropriate literature for secondary students. It provides the "strategies for living" many young adult readers seek from their reading, and it is written to be accessible to young adults emotionally and cognitively—as readers still developing their reading skills. Because it speaks to students' needs and interests, this literature is more likely to motivate young adults to want to read: witness the immense appeal of the Harry Potter series. Second, teachers, building on their students' willingness to read, can better help their students meet the goals of the reading program, using such texts to help students practice reading for different purposes and other skills important in the curriculum.

YA literature provides the "strategies for living" that many young adult readers seek from their reading.

Young adult author Richard Peck, in a collection of essays titled *Love and Death at the Mall* (1994), defines the genre in which he works by saying, "Young adult novels test the boundaries . . . leading to the subtext of all our books: the responsibility for the consequences of actions" (p. 159). Walter Dean Myers, another honored writer of YA novels, says that, in general, "Literature gives strategies for living" (personal communication, November 22, 1997). And Sandy Asher, also an author of books for young adults, concurs, stating

> Generally, adults choose books that reflect and reinforce attitudes they already hold. Young adult readers, on the other hand, are actively searching for ideas, information, and values to incorporate into their personalities and into their lives. The books they read become a very real part of them. (1992, p. 82)

Stotan! is a good example of why a young man like Richie is drawn to such works. Walker and his friends learn that their teammate, Jeff, is dying of leukemia. They do not know how to handle this news; they are uncomfortable with Jeff and with each other as they try to explore how to interact with him. Readers learn along with Walker what it is Jeff most wants: "Jeff made it clear to us that all we can do for him is be there if he needs us and swim like unlimited hydroplanes at State" (Crutcher, 1986, p. 151). Later their coach tells them:

> The point is, the Dragon is here and he seems to have come in the form of Death. He's ugly. And, guys, what you learned about yourselves during Stotan Week can help you here. The magic wasn't in gritting your teeth and enduring the pain with no show of emotion. It was in letting go: accepting reality; what *is* as they say. That's the only way you'll find strength to deal with this. (p. 169)

And so, as Richie identifies with Walker and his athletic friends, he too may come to develop some strategies for coping with the unexpected curve balls life throws him.

YA literature is, in general, developmentally appropriate.

Authors such as Myers, Asher, and Crutcher seem to understand intuitively the stages of reading development outlined more than forty years ago by Margaret Early (1960), but which often are not honored by teachers and curriculum workers. According to Early, children begin their lives as readers by reading with "unconscious enjoyment," gobbling up books voraciously—though often returning to the same books again and again. As they mature, by third or fourth grade these readers have developed the speed and skill necessary to move forward into more complex texts, and they also begin to develop the ability to lose themselves in a book, to feel as though time has stopped and that reality exists only as the pages unfold.

At this stage, Early (1960) finds, readers of upper elementary and middle school age become more adept at adding to their own delight by beginning to demand an internal, logical consistency within the texts they choose, by starting to reject stereotypes, and by searching through books for insights about their own potential futures: What will middle school hold for me? What is it like to go on a date? How can I be myself when my parents continue to control my activities? Therefore, middle school readers will appreciate the fact that Woodson's *I Hadn't Meant to Tell You This* (1994) pairs a white girl from an impoverished, abusive family with a middle-class, high-achieving African American girl in a friendship from which each learns valuable lessons about loyalty and self-preservation. And, even while they are laughing over the scene in *Alice in Rapture, Sort Of* (1989), in which Naylor describes the mechanics and logistics of a first kiss, middle school students will be comforted to know that they are not alone in wondering how you breathe or what to do about gum at such a time. High school readers, on the other hand, will follow with eagerness the adventures of Draper's *Romiette and Julio* (1999), with its allusions to the Shakespeare play and its dreamlike fantasy elements, because the novel can teach them something about the nature of love and destiny.

Early goes on to suggest that the mature reader, "with the artist, digs at the wellsprings of life" (1960, p. 166). Building on Early's theory, other scholars such as Donelson and Nilsen find that by senior high, good readers become capable of "venturing beyond themselves," or of feeling "concern for philosophical problems" (2001, p. 53). They read to assess their place in the larger world by exploring other places, times, and situations through vicarious literary experiences. They read to find out more about how relationships work, how an individual's values affect his or her behavior, what the range of ethical perspectives might be about a particular issue, and thus more about their own take on life in general. Therefore, teachers might want to give them a book such as Klass's *California Blue* (1994), in which John, having discovered that the forest his father's logging company is about to cut is the last remaining habitat of an endangered butterfly, has a decision to make. Will he side with his family and friends and thus condemn the beautiful creature to extinction, or will he help to protect it—and risk shutting down his family's mill, the main place of employment in his town? Or, Cooney's *Burning Up* (1999) can take older readers on a journey of discovery into the past with Macey, as she learns about prejudice, racism, and their lingering effects that reach into the lives of her family in the present day.

Mature readers read for a variety of reasons, from the aesthetic to the sociological. At the same time, they constantly move back and forth among the stages of reading, using a variety of skills and approaches depending on their purpose for reading at any given point. Good teachers recognize that their secondary school classes will hold readers of different stages of development with different reading interests and different backgrounds of experience on which to draw to make sense of a text. As Hynds (1990) concludes from her studies of readers, if these varying reading interests and abilities are not taken into account, we will lose our students as potential members of a literacy community. That is what happened to Richie before he was introduced to *Stotan!*

YA literature meets the needs of its readers; therefore, this literature is more likely to motivate students to want to read and to work hard at reading.

In general, then, the primary value of using YA literature within the secondary reading program is that it is more likely to provide students with a motivation to want to read. If students are not willing to actually pick up a book and open its pages, then teachers will have difficulty attending to any other curricular goals related to reading. National Assessment of Educational Progress (NAEP) results from 1994 indicate that motivation to read, and the related increase in the practice of reading skill, does affect reading proficiency levels. We know that eighth and twelfth graders who read more than five pages a day have higher scores than their peers, so teachers need to find texts that will make students *want* to turn more than five pages a day—books such as Marsden's *Letters from the Inside* (1994), an epistolary novel in which the two young female correspondents gradually reveal more and more about themselves and the grim situations in which they live. This story creates suspense about girls who seem, on the surface, to be typical adolescents and so pull readers into their worlds.

Teachers can use YA literature to help their students learn to read for different purposes and to address other skills typically addressed in the secondary reading program.

Because it comes in every known genre, YA literature can be used by teachers to help students learn to read for the three primary purposes assessed by the NAEP: (1) reading to gain information, (2) reading to perform a task, and (3) reading for literary experience. Teachers might ask students to skim Galt's *Up to the Plate* (1995) in quest of information about the women's baseball league of the 1940s, or to read a work of fiction such as Reuter's *The Boys from St. Petri* (1994) to develop a different perspective on World War II. They might have students scan Krizmanic's *A Teen's Guide to Going Vegetarian* (1994) for specific clues about how to become a vegetarian without antagonizing their friends or their parents. Students can benefit from reading books such as Mori's *Shizuko's Daughter* (1993), about a young woman coming of age in Japan in the shadow of her mother's suicide, or Cofer's *An Island Like You* (1995), a collection of interrelated short stories about life in the barrios of New Jersey. Such works can not only give their students cross-cultural perspectives, but they can also provide an aesthetic literary experience through, for instance, the poetic, shimmering qualities of Mori's prose as she describes the role of color and light in Shizuko's world, or the dialect and gritty descriptive phrases that characterize Cofer's work.

Once students do become excited about a text, teachers can work on developmentally appropriate skills such as vocabulary development, grammatical understanding, and other language concepts. Bushman and Bushman (1997, p. 6) suggest that students reading Paterson's *The Great Gilly Hopkins* (1979) should compare and contrast the vocabulary and syntax of the down-to-earth and loving Maime Trotter with the flowery, highly literate speech patterns of Mr. Randolf, discussing in general how an individual's language choices reflect his or her personality and values. Again, the 1994 NAEP findings support the use of YA literature in the reading program as a tool in developing such skills: We know that eighth and twelfth graders who are asked to explain at least once a week what they read and to discuss various interpretations of what they read have higher reading proficiency levels.

YA literature can also introduce secondary readers to the artistic elements used by writers of any great literature and thus serve as a bridge to more sophisticated texts.

Quality YA literature demonstrates the artistic elements and craftsmanship characteristic of the true artist; therefore, YA literature can be used to help students understand the nature of literature as an art form just as well as the traditional "great books." Students reading Joan Lowry Nixon's excellent mysteries for young adults can develop their understanding of "the form of the narrative, chapters, rising action, climax, and resolution," as well as "foreshadowing, flashbacks, and point of view," thereby also building "the needed schemata for the genre" (Pavonetti, 1996, p. 54). When secondary readers can relate to the characters emotionally, they are more able to begin to appreciate literature as an art and to start to recognize how good writers craft language.

Twenty years ago Robert Small (1977) argued in "The Junior Novel and the Art of Literature" that YA literature is analogous to "working models" employed in the education of engineers. By virtue of its elegant simplicity, "[t]he well-written junior novel, in contrast [to the adult novel], invites, welcomes students to meet it as equals. They can become real authorities on the literary craft" and "can establish a critical relationship" (p. 57) to titles such as *Stotan!*, *California Blue*, or *An Island Like You.*

Titles written specifically for and about young adults deal with issues ranging from how to survive in the workforce, as in Strasser's *Workin' for Peanuts* (1983), to how to take a stand in support of a friend in the face of a community's homophobia, as in Garden's *The Year They Burned the Books* (1999), to how to deal with being learning disabled, as in Jack Gantos's *Joey Pigza Loses Control* (2000). These works pull students into their worlds and motivate them to *want* to "make meaning from text." Then they can be used to help these readers understand the nature of the artists' craft in creating such worlds, thereby serving teachers and students well as they pursue the goals of the reading program. Thus, when students later encounter the stylistic, structural, or thematic complexities of *As I Lay Dying*, they have a handle on how to wrestle with such a text, having cut their literary teeth on titles more readily accessible.

YA literature can be used by teachers seeking to tailor reading programs to the needs of particular students who read with diverse levels of skill and who come from diverse cultural backgrounds and experiences.

YA literature can serve as an alternative to the anthology-based instructional reading programs that make it difficult for teachers to individualize their programs. Roe, Stoodt, and Burns, in *Secondary School Literacy Instruction: The Content Areas* (1998), point out that secondary school instruction continues to be highly textbook based. But a reliance on textbooks makes it difficult to cover content in more than a superficial way and also makes it difficult for the teacher to individualize instruction. Using text sets of books of any sort, but particularly books written for young adults, is one way teachers can accommodate the needs and interests of a heterogeneous group of students. For instance, imagine that Richie, a fairly unskilled reader, was in a class with my friend the sophisticated reader and future Phi Beta Kappa. The teacher, to deal with the issue of point of view and the variety of narrative options available to an author, might introduce several titles to the class. Zindel's *The Pigman* (1968), which alternates the voices of Lorraine and John in telling the tale of their friendship with the elderly Mr. Pignati, might appeal to Richie, while the more sophisticated reader could read Avi's *Nothing but the Truth* (1991), a "documentary novel" that includes dialogues, fragments of memos, excerpts from diaries, letters, phone conversations, and reports without any clear narrative thread as it explores the politics of high schools and the flaws of our educational system. During class discussion of their reading experiences, both readers will become more adept at recognizing the ways in which the author's choice of narrative voice affects the reader's relationship to the text. Neither reader, however, should become frustrated by the level of complexity in the text with which he or she is dealing.

Teachers can find titles to which students of all abilities can relate. Students with special needs who have difficulty reading, as well as those gifted students who read with ease, can "find themselves" in YA books. Both groups can satisfy their desire to know more about what the future might hold, and thus what the consequences of particular choices and decisions might be. Adler's *Kiss the Clown* (1986) and the nonfiction work *Dyslexia* (1997) by Moragne show the student with reading disabilities that he or she is not alone. Titles such as *Midnight Hour Encores* (1986) by Brooks, *Welcome to the Ark* (1996) by Tolan, and *Shizuko's Daughter* (1993) by Mori are about young adults struggling to make sense of their giftedness. Hesser's *Kissing Doorknobs* (1998), about what life is like for a young person with obsessive/compulsive disorder, is just one example of a title that can be used to help students realize that others share their experiences.

Teachers can also use a variety of YA texts to provide ways in to literature for students from diverse cultural backgrounds. There is now a body of YA literature that reflects the diverse experiences of members of various minority cultures within the United States, as well as of diverse cultures throughout the world. Writers such as Walter Dean Myers, Marie Lee, Lensey Namioka, Gary Soto, and Jean Okimoto create characters who are particularly important to students who share those characters' heritages. As Frankson (1990) states, "To develop a positive image of their roles as valuable members of society, minority youth need to see themselves represented in good literature, both in their classrooms and on the library shelves" (p. 30). Reading such books might also help make us and our students face the facts about the presence of racism and ethnocentricity in our lives and our society, as well as become more tolerant and appreciative of diverse perspectives. For instance, *Frankie's Story* (1989), a trilogy by Martin Waddell writing as Catherine Sefton, is about a young woman coming of age surrounded by the chaos of the religious and political strife of contemporary Belfast. This story makes the complexities of the situation in Ireland much more real and even understandable to a young person unfamiliar with it, because it is so easy to feel for the main character as she comes to realize she can become herself only if she leaves her family and familiar situation, however difficult the move.

As students read books about young people who are dealing with issues of identity, career choice, place within the family, or development of intimate relationships, but doing so in cultural contexts different from those with which they are familiar, they can also begin to appreciate that an art form both reflects and in some ways creates the culture out of which it is generated. Discussing what terms such as *classical, truth, adulthood, love,* or *wilderness* mean when used in YA literature from other countries or when written into texts by individuals of Native American heritage, such as *Morning Girl* (1992) by Michael Dorris, allows adolescent readers to better understand the pluralistic nature of the world and the nature of text as cultural artifact.

At the same time, reading such books helps young adults begin to understand how we define ourselves in relationship to the norms of our particular culture. Discussing such books can then facilitate consideration and redefinition of those boundaries against which a sense of self is formed and tested. These kinds of discussions require the critical and creative thinking skills that are often cited as important within the developmental reading program.

In addition to the formal use of YA literature in their programs, teachers can encourage independent reading by surrounding their students with classrooms filled with intriguing titles students can access for self-selected reading. If the Richies of our schools do not have a way to get their hands on books such as *Stotan!*, they will not be able to read them. As long ago as 1976, Fader discussed the value of saturating classrooms with paperback books so that students would have difficulty *not* picking up a novel or poetry anthology and starting to browse its pages. Atwell (1987), Rief (1992), and others continue to advocate the importance of providing students with books that look appealing and the time to read on their own.

YA literature can be used throughout the curriculum so that students develop content-area reading skills and the ability to make interdisciplinary connections.

Asking students to read a variety of texts within the context of various content areas is an important component of a reading program designed to help students develop fluency. Using YA texts across the curriculum will allow students to practice their reading and to see the value of their work in reading class from a broader perspective. Rather than reading only a chapter from a history text on the civil rights movement, students also might read a novel such as Curtis's *The Watsons Go to Birmingham—1963* (1995), in which the effects of the Birmingham church bombings are illustrated through the story of a family who lived through them. Beake's *Song of Be* (1993) can be used to illustrate the political realities and dynamics of developing nations such as Namibia. A book such as *The Night Room* (1995) by Goldman provokes discussion about the ethics of new technologies such as virtual reality games, while Pausewang's *Fall-Out* (1994) can be used in science units to study nuclear fallout and related environmental issues. Naylor's *The Year of the Gopher* (1987) could enhance a consumer math class because the novel centers on high school students struggling to deal with personal financial situations. Even though first-year foreign-language students probably do not have the requisite skill to read a book in the original language, teachers can ask them to read Boissard's *A Matter of Feeling* (1977) translated from the French, or *Who Killed Christopher?* (1980) by German author Korschunow, in order to make connections between their own lives and those of their contemporaries in other countries. And nonfiction titles written specifically for young adults can also supplement content-area teaching. *Big Star Fallin' Mama: Five Women in Black Music* (1995) by Jones, Johnson's *Science on the Ice: An Antarctic Journal* (1995), or Freedman's *Lincoln: A Photobiography* (1987) all deserve a place in the music, science, or history classroom. The point is to surround students with inviting texts throughout their school day, and to help them see how reading offers insights into the human dimensions and relevance of a curriculum from which they might otherwise feel disconnected.

Infusing YA Literature into Secondary Reading Programs

Teachers who are knowledgeable about their students' needs and interests and who understand the reasons why YA literature appeals to them can use this literature, written specifically for and about adolescents, as a bridge between their students' world(s) and the worlds of the texts most often found in the literature curriculum, regardless of whether that curriculum is organized by genre, theme, or chronology. Research suggests that good readers read best when they have adequate prior knowledge to make sense of a text and are helped to organize and use that knowledge base effectively (Anderson and Pearson, 1984; Valeri-Gold, 1986). The four volumes of Kaywell's series *Adolescent Literature as a Complement to the Classics* (1993–2000) show teachers how to apply this research. These volumes provide wonderful insights into how to pair a YA text with a classic text in order to tap students' experiences and backgrounds, thus enhancing their understanding of both works.

Using YA Literature in a Genre-Based Literature Program

The literature curriculum at the ninth- or tenth-grade level is often organized as a study of literary genres. Students read novels, short stories, poetry, epics, and plays, determining the defining criteria and analyzing the ways in which constituent elements of each genre interact to form a whole. "A&P" by John Updike (1959) is one short story often anthologized because of its youthful protagonist, Sammy, a nineteen-year-old grocery store clerk who, for reasons not quite clear to himself, defends three adolescent girls who come into the store in their bathing suits in violation of store policy. Unfortunately for Sammy, the form of his protest against the way his manager has treated the girls is to quit— and the girls do not even know he does so. The last line of the story is in Sammy's voice: "I knew how difficult life would be from then on."

Today's students can still relate to Sammy. They understand his vague desire to "do something," and they ache for him as he begins to realize the consequences of his action. But the setting is a difficult one for modern readers to connect with. The actions of the three young women no longer seem risqué, and Sammy's attitude toward them reflects a chauvinistic view of women that some contemporary female readers find off-putting. Pairing Sammy's story with almost any of the titles from *No Easy Answers: Short Stories about Teenagers Making Tough Choices* (1997), edited by Don Gallo, would allow students to consider the thematic issues of choice and consequence as they compare Sammy's decisions to those of the more contemporary stories' protagonists. In particular, "Bliss at the Burger Bar" (1997) by Louise Plummer would be a useful companion to "A&P." In both stories, setting is important, and both main characters are struggling to figure out what it means to be a grown-up and to take responsibility for both oneself and others. In Plummer's story, however, the chauvinism of one male character allows him to beat his girlfriend, Hannah, to the point that her face "looks like roadkill," and then Bliss has the very real-world problem of trying to help her friend, who wants to make excuses for the boy's behavior. The nature of the first-person narrator and its effect on the reader could be discussed, especially since in one case the narrator is male and in the other, female. Bliss has definite goals; Sammy is vague about where his life is headed. In both stories, the authors develop these clearly defined characters through dialogue, interior monologue, and action in a very short amount of space, so students could be led to better appreciate the constraints under which a short-story writer works. Additionally, both authors also write novels. It would be interesting for students to compare how successful each author is in each genre—a project that would lead naturally into an exploration of the nature of the novel as a literary form.

Similar pairings of YA texts with those often used to teach other genres can easily be developed. Teachers can foster students' appreciation for the craft of language and genre by including in the curriculum texts addressed specifically to a young adult audience, giving students more direct access to the conventions of language, structure, and story, and thereby helping teenage readers see the ways in which the nature of genres affects the work of the author regardless of his or her intended audience.

Using YA Literature in a Thematically Based Literature Program

Often, literature curricula are organized around key themes that transcend boundaries of time and space. One of my student teachers recently was working within such a curriculum, teaching a unit titled "Call It Courage." The curriculum called for topics such as the meaning of integrity, the nature of a hero as a concept in both everyday life and in literature, and personal versus societal perceptions of courage; the primary text the student teacher was to use was Crane's *The Red Badge of Courage* (1894/1982). This particular young woman was less than excited about the prospect of spending a significant amount of time on Crane's novel because it was one she herself had found boring as an eleventh-grade student, although she noted that having studied Crane's poetry in college, she had a better appreciation for the philosophical and historical contexts that shaped his work and had found the novel more interesting from a psychological perspective when she read it prior to starting her unit. But she feared that her students would respond as she had when she was sixteen. Fortunately, we found Pam Cole's (1995) essay "Bridging *The Red Badge of Courage* with Six Related Young Adult Novels." Cole outlines the plot similarities and analyzes the thematic connections between six novels published for young adults set in varying war-time periods—from the American Revolution through the Vietnam War—and describes the use of literature circles as a strategy for promoting students' ability to deal with the character development, symbolism, imagery, and naturalistic philosophy in Crane's novel by using the more contemporary pieces as a touchstone.

Building on Cole's suggestions, the student teacher used Paulsen's *Soldier's Heart* (1998; Civil War), Cormier's *Heroes* (1998; World War II), Westall's *Gulf* (1996; Gulf War), and Mead's *Adem's Cross* (1996; Balkan conflict) as starting points for discussing war and how courage is defined in times of national conflict. From there, she provided students with a list of titles that develop the theme of courage in other situations. Cooney's *Burning Up* (1999), about a young woman who takes on her community in an effort to right wrongs based on the prejudices of its inhabitants in times past, and Hesser's *Kissing Door-knobs* (1998), about a young woman dealing with the reality of her ob-sessive/compulsive disorder, are just two examples from the list. By the time the students had finished the unit, they had held interesting discussions on questions ranging from "How can the 'good guys' and 'bad guys' be identified and defined?" to "What is the relationship of innocence to courage? Is it possible to remain innocent and still exhibit courage?" All the students read *The Red Badge of Courage* and at least two other novels, so their discussions were rich with references that crossed literary and historical time periods and that connected the im-portant themes of Crane's work to their own lives.

Using YA Literature in Surveys of American, British, or World Literature

English curricula at the eleventh- and twelfth-grade levels are often or-ganized to provide students with a historical overview of the literature of the United States, Great Britain, or the world. In American literature courses, students begin with sermons such as those by Jonathan Ed-wards and move slowly forward in time, arriving at the 1920s and Fitzgerald's *The Great Gatsby* by the end of the school year, if they're lucky. In British literature surveys, students march steadily forward in time from *Beowulf* to Shakespeare to the Romantic poets and Hardy, and sometimes manage to fit in a "modern" writer such as James Joyce. It is even more difficult to provide a useful historical survey of world litera-ture because the literary heritage is longer and more complex as readers go back in time to the oral traditions of various cultures and attempt to learn, through reading, about the history of world literature from Euro-pean, Asian, Indian, African, and South American perspectives.

Faced with difficult language, unfamiliar settings, and charac-ters who seem to live lives unrelated to their own, students often shut down, taking notes on the texts instead of actually reading them. As Vogel and Zancanella (1991) note in their analysis of the literary lives of four adolescents, most teenagers faced with such a curriculum lose interest in school reading. While they may have rich reading lives out-side of school, "literature in school means absorbing the viewpoint of the teacher" (p. 57). In a similar study, Sullivan (1991) describes how the students with whom she talked turned to the reading of "Mr. Cliff" so that they would know what the teachers wanted them to know about texts presented for "study" and yet continue to have time for their own, more pleasurable, reading choices.

Again, it is possible to help bridge the gap between students' experiences and perceptions and the worlds of traditional survey course texts by pairing such texts with YA titles that can be compared thematically, stylistically, or historically. Stover and Zitlow's "Is the Dream Still Possible? Using Young Adult Literature from Diverse Hispanic Perspectives to Illuminate Themes in *Don Quixote*" (1997) demonstrates how to combine YA texts and a classic work in ways that illuminate a variety of themes: "Battling Windmills or the Monstrous Giants of Poverty and Prejudice," "Pride and Persistence," "Re-Creating Self," "Companions in Battles," "Reality and Fantasy," and "Living in Dreams amidst Grim Reality with an Imagination That Keeps the Self Alive." In similar fashion, in "Race, Racism, and Racial Harmony: Using Classic and Young Adult Literature to Teach *Othello, the Moor of Venice*," Christenbury (1996) outlines strategies for using YA literature to prompt discussion of interracial friendships/relationships before reading Shakespeare's play. In these books with contemporary settings and modern protagonists, the authors deal with issues of racial identity and the ways in which race influences an individual's place in society and his or her values and fears. Teachers who favor the classics and believe in their importance in helping students develop a sense of cultural heritage will be pleased with the balanced perspective offered in these essays.

Teaching with YA Literature

Regardless of the organizational structure of the curriculum, teachers using YA literature to enhance the reading program should employ pedagogical strategies that will help their students interact in meaningful ways with these texts. The chapters in this volume describe techniques such as literature circles, student-led discussion strategies, literature-based cooperative and collaborative activities, writing as a learning tool and the related use of reading logs and journals; these and others are all strategies that encourage student involvement in the reading process and foster the development of higher-level thinking skills. The professional resources listed at the end of this chapter are all useful for learning more about these strategies.

Conclusion

Young adult literature such as Crutcher's *Stotan!* helps accomplish the goals of secondary reading programs because high school readers can easily identify with, and so come to care about, the characters and their situations—to the point that they want to talk about these "people" with someone else at 10:00 P.M.! Now that Richie has gotten to know Walker, Nortie, and Jeff, he has told his tutor that he wants to meet more of Crutcher's characters, and he has asked her to recommend other "good books with real people." A reluctant and "poor" reader, Richie is now seeking out books to read. As he practices his reading with books about individuals to whom he can relate, his fluency and comprehension and other related skills should also improve.

My lawyer friend did not have any kind of "reading problem," but her motivation to read was squashed by the demands of continually reading assigned books about people in situations unlike those in her own emotional experience; gradually she began to perceive reading as a chore. Reading became something to complete on a "to do" list instead of a pleasurable activity that could enrich her life. While she learned to take notes, analyze texts, and write papers, and while her vocabulary, comprehension, and other reading skills developed, she became, for many years, a "nonreader" except when she had to open a text for an assignment.

Giving YA literature a central place in secondary reading programs should be an important strategy for teachers eager to foster in their students a love of reading that will last a lifetime. In *Memoirs of a Bookbat* (1994), Lasky introduces us to Harper, a young woman struggling to differentiate herself from her parents and their increasingly conservative religious beliefs. Harper finds solace in books, and she is eloquent about the value of reading in her life:

> Just that afternoon at the library story time, Nancy had read a beautiful poem about a baby bat being born. It described bats' "sharp ears, their sharp teeth, their quick sharp faces." It told how they soared and looped through the night, how they listened by sending out what the poetry called "shining needlepoints of sound." Bats live by hearing. I realized, standing in front of Nettie right then, that when I read I am like a bat soaring and swooping through the night, skimming across the treetops to find my way through the densest forest in the darkest night. I listen to the shining needlepoints of sound in every book I read. I am no bookworm. I am a bookbat. (pp. 31–32)

While helping teachers meet all the secondary goals of reading programs, the use of young adult literature uniquely promotes its primary goal: the creation of lifelong readers. Teachers who understand Hunter's "real-life issues that draw readers to novels or condition their choices of reading material" (1990, p. 79) will offer their secondary readers young adult literature as a way to help them satisfy their hunger to learn about themselves, their futures, and their worlds.

References

Professional Resources

Anderson, R. C., & Pearson, P. D. (1984). A schema-theoretic view of basic processes in reading. In P. D. Pearson, R. Barr, M. L. Kamil, & P. Mosenthal (Eds.), *Handbook of reading research* (Vol. 1., pp. 255–91). White Plains, NY: Longman.

Asher, Sandy. (1992). What about now? What about here? What about me? In V. Monseau & G. Salvner (Eds.), *Reading their world: The young adult novel in the classroom* (pp. 77–82). Portsmouth, NH: Boynton/Cook.

Atwell, N. (1987). *In the middle: Writing, reading, and learning with adolescents.* Upper Montclair, NJ: Boynton/Cook.

Bates, R. (1995). Personal reading histories: A useful tool in the effort to map reading communities. In M. Grosman (Ed.), *American literature for non-American readers: Cross-cultural perspectives on American literature* (pp. 113–21). New York: Peter Lang.

Brown, J. E., & Stephens, E. C. (1995). *Teaching young adult literature: Sharing the connection.* Belmont, CA: Wadsworth.

Bushman, J., & Bushman, K. (1997). *Using young adult literature in the English classroom* (2nd ed.). Upper Saddle River, NJ: Merrill.

Christenbury, L. (1996). Race, racism, and racial harmony: Using classic and young adult literature to teach *Othello, the Moor of Venice.* In J. Kaywell (Ed.), *Adolescent literature as a complement to the classics, Vol. III* (pp. 93–104). Norwood, MA: Christopher Gordon.

Cole, P. B. (1995). Bridging *The Red Badge of Courage* with six related young adult novels. In J. Kaywell (Ed.), *Adolescent literature as a complement to the classics, Vol. II* (pp. 21–39). Norwood, MA: Christopher Gordon.

Donelson, K., & Nilsen, A. P. (2001). *Literature for today's young adults* (6th ed.). New York: Longman.

Early, M. (1960). Stages of growth in literary appreciation. *English Journal, 49*(3), 161–67.

Fader, D. (1976). *The new hooked on books.* New York: Berkley.

Frankson, M. S. (1990). Chicano literature for young adults: An annotated bibliography. *English Journal, 79*(1), 30–38.

Hunter, J. P. (1990). *Before novels: The cultural context of eighteenth-century English fiction.* New York: Norton.

Hynds, S. (1990). Reading as a social event: Comprehension and response in the text, classroom and world. In D. Bogdan & S. B. Straw (Eds.), *Beyond communication: Reading comprehension and criticism* (pp. 237–56). Portsmouth, NH: Boynton/Cook.

Kaywell, J. (Ed.). (1993–2000). *Adolescent literature as a complement to the classics: Volumes 1–4.* Norwood, MA: Christopher Gordon.

Pavonetti, L. M. (1996). Joan Lowry Nixon: The grande dame of young adult mystery. *Journal of Adolescent & Adult Literacy, 39,* 454–61.

Peck, R. (1994). *Love and death at the mall: Teaching and writing for the literate young.* New York: Delacorte Press.

Results from the NAEP 1994 Reading Assessment-At-A-Glance. NAEP Home Page: www/ed.gov:80/NCES/NAEP/y25flk/rbro.shtml. (No date.)

Rief, L. (1992). *Seeking diversity: Language arts with adolescents.* Portsmouth, NH: Heinemann.

Roe, B., Stoodt, B. D., & Burns, P. C. (1998). *Secondary school literacy instruction: The content areas* (6th ed.). Boston: Houghton Mifflin.

Small, R. (1977). The junior novel and the art of literature. *English Journal, 66*(7), 56–59.

Stover, L., & Zitlow, C. (1997). Is the dream still possible? Using young adult literature from diverse Hispanic perspectives to illuminate themes in *Don Quixote.* In J. Kaywell (Ed.), *Adolescent literature as a complement to the classics, Vol. 3* (pp. 137–58). Norwood, MA: Christopher Gordon.

Sullivan, A. M. (1991). The natural reading life: A high-school anomaly. *English Journal, 80*(6), 40–46.

Valeri-Gold, M. (1986). Previewing: A directed reading-thinking activity. *Reading Horizons, 27,* 123–26.

Vogel, M., & Zancanella, D. (1991). The story world of adolescents in and out of the classroom. *English Journal, 80*(6), 54–60.

Young Adult Literature

Adler, C. S. (1986). *Kiss the clown.* New York: Clarion Books.

Avi. (1991). *Nothing but the truth.* New York: Orchard Books.

Beake, L. (1993). *Song of be.* New York: Holt.

Boissard, J. (1977). *A matter of feeling.* (M. Feeley, Trans.). Boston: Little, Brown.

Brooks, B. (1986). *Midnight hour encores.* New York: Harper & Row.

Bruchac, J. (2000). *Sacajawea: The story of Bird Woman and the Lewis and Clark expedition.* San Diego: Silver Whistle.

Cofer, J. O. (1995). *An island like you: Stories of the barrio.* New York: Orchard Books.

Cooney, C. (1999). *Burning up.* New York: Delacorte Press.

Cormier, R. (1998). *Heroes.* New York: Delacorte Press.

Crane, S. (1982). *The red badge of courage.* Pleasantville, NY: Reader's Digest Association. (Original work published 1894)

Crutcher, C. (1986). *Stotan!* New York: Greenwillow Press.

Curtis, C. P. (1995). *The Watsons go to Birmingham—1963.* New York: Delacorte Press.

Dorris, M. (1992). *Morning girl.* New York: Hyperion.

Draper, S. (1999). *Romiette and Julio.* New York: Atheneum.

Draper, S. (1994). *Tears of a tiger.* New York: Atheneum.

Faulkner, W. (1964). *As I lay dying.* New York: Vintage Books.

Freedman, R. (1987). *Lincoln: A photobiography.* New York: Clarion Books.

Gallo, D. (Ed.). (1997). *No easy answers: Short stories about teenagers making tough choices.* New York: Delacorte Press.

Galt, M. F. (1995). *Up to the plate: The All American Girls Professional Baseball League.* Minneapolis, MN: Lerner.

Gantos, J. (2000). *Joey Pigza loses control.* New York: Farrar, Straus and Giroux.

Garden, N. (1999). *The year they burned the books.* New York: Farrar, Straus and Giroux.

Golding, W. (1955). *Lord of the flies.* New York: Coward-McCann.

Goldman, E. M. (1995). *The night room.* New York: Viking.

Hardy, T. (1983). *Tess of the D'Urbervilles.* New York: Clarendon.

Hesser, T. S. (1998). *Kissing doorknobs.* New York: Delacorte Press.

Johnson, R. (1995). *Science on the ice: An Antarctic journal.* Minneapolis, MN: Lerner.

Jones, H. (1995). *Big star fallin' mama: Five women in black music.* New York: Viking.

Klass, D. (1994). *California blue.* New York: Scholastic.

Knowles, J. (1960). *A separate peace.* New York: Macmillan.

Korschunow, I. (1980). *Who killed Christopher?* New York: Collins.

Krizmanic, J. (1994). *A teen's guide to going vegetarian.* New York: Viking.

Lasky, K. (1994). *Memoirs of a bookbat.* San Diego: Harcourt Brace.

Marsden, J. (1994). *Letters from the inside.* Boston: Houghton Mifflin.

Mead, A. (1996). *Adem's cross.* New York: Farrar, Straus and Giroux.

Moragne, W. (1997). *Dyslexia.* Brookfield, CT: Millbrook Press.

Mori, K. (1993). *Shizuko's daughter.* New York: Holt.

Naylor, P. R. (1989). *Alice in rapture, sort of.* New York: Atheneum.

Naylor, P. R. (1987). *The year of the gopher.* New York: Atheneum.

Paterson, K. (1979). *The great Gilly Hopkins.* New York: Avon Books.

Paulsen, G. (1998). *Soldier's heart: A novel of the Civil War.* New York: Delacorte Press.

Pausewang, G. (1994). *Fall-out.* (P. Crampton, Trans.). London: Viking.

Plummer, L. (1997). Bliss at the burger bar. In D. Gallo (Ed.), *No easy answers: Short stories about young teenagers making tough choices* (pp. 27–42). New York: Delacorte Press.

Reuter, B. (1994). *The boys from St. Petri.* (Anthea Bell, Trans.). New York: Dutton.

Rodowsky, C. (1985). *Julie's daughter.* New York: Farrar, Straus and Giroux.

Salinger, J. D. (1951). *Catcher in the rye.* Boston: Little, Brown.

Sefton, C. (1989). *Frankie's story.* London: Methuen.

Seymour, K. (1990). How I found me by reading. In R. Bates (Ed.), *I took Intro. to Lit. and this is all I got out of it: An anthology of student essays* (pp. 1–5). St. Mary's City: St. Mary's College of Maryland.

Strasser, T. (1983). *Workin' for peanuts.* New York: Delacorte Press.

Tolan, S. (1996). *Welcome to the ark.* New York: Morrow.

Updike, J. (1959). A&P. In *Pigeonfeathers and other stories.* Greenwich, CT: Fawcett.

Westall, R. (1996). *Gulf.* New York: Scholastic.

Woodson, J. (1994). *I hadn't meant to tell you this.* New York: Delacorte Press.

Zindel, P. (1968). *The pigman.* New York: Bantam.

10 Picture Books in the High School English Classroom

Carolyn Lott
University of Montana

Matching young adult literature with high school reading so that students can grasp concepts and develop understandings seems to be an accepted practice among many high school teachers; several resources support using young adult literature with classics to add depth and variety as well as enjoyment to the secondary English classroom (Herz, 1996; Kaywell, 1993, 1995, 1997, 2000; Stover, Chapter 9 of this volume). But not many secondary teachers, even those of English, have made it a practice to incorporate children's literature, specifically picture books, as part of the instructional materials for their classes. Literacy growth as a result of reading children's literature need not stop at the end of the fourth or fifth grades; nor does students' appreciation of children's literature diminish in higher grades (Ammon & Sherman, 1996; Benedict & Carlisle, 1992; Shively, 1993). In fact, children's picture books can be used in a variety of ways in the high school classroom to enhance the reading practices of older students:

- to introduce literary elements, concepts, and study topics
- to model writing style and genre
- to appreciate the sophistication of succinct, targeted language
- to practice specific content-area reading strategies in new and familiar pieces of literature
- to connect print and illustration in media literacy
- to demonstrate critical theory applications in literature
- to challenge, enrich, and connect high school literature with quality children's literature

Notice I have not mentioned that children's literature should be used to *remediate* high school students' reading skills. I do not want to suggest that children's literature is solely for students with literacy problems; rather, this chapter illustrates that picture books can be used effectively with older students for developing higher-level reading skills associated with high school reading requirements. Children's literature can be utilized at the secondary level to enhance students' thinking and reading skills by

- offering enticing books for students who know how to read but choose not to
- substituting shorter books for students who prefer not to read longer texts
- contributing understandable language to help develop inferences, concepts, or generalizations
- presenting multiple opportunities for analyzing, synthesizing, and evaluating what they read
- giving vocabulary and background for comprehending information in content-specific nonfiction formats, helping students succeed in their classes across all areas of the curriculum

As a high school English teacher, Bruce Pirie (1997) declared that the most exciting classes he ever conducted were based on examining a short story or poem—a short, live, on-the-spot reading—and "sharing the excitement and discovery of collaboratively building a reading" (p. 34). Children's literature beautifully fulfills the literary requirements to duplicate with all students Pirie's experience. He also maintained that "[w]e need to unlock reading processes, making them available for students' understanding, practice, and experimentation, encouraging them to become aware of themselves as readers" (p. 34). Quality picture books can be just the key to model and demonstrate for older students their own reading processes.

Defining Children's Literature/Picture Books

Children's literature usually refers to books written for the younger child, from the first books a child sees and hears read to the longer books with chapters read by students in the upper elementary grades (Norton, 1999). The growing body of literature, over 9,000 titles published yearly, includes picture books, a subset of children's literature. Picture books have illustrations or art that add content and facilitate interpretation of the text; the illustrations and text in a picture book contribute to the enjoyment and literary growth of any reader. Picture books include sophisticated and sometimes complicated stories written for younger children that can be used successfully with high school students. The "children's" part of some picture books is often a misnomer: levels and depths of understanding possible in publications targeted to younger readers enhance the reading and interpretative skills of any reader. Therefore, picture books in this chapter refer to the books that depend at least equally, sometimes more, on illustrations as on text for presenting story elements, literary elements, and content information to its readers.

Literary Elements, Concepts, and Study Topics

High school students of English language arts focus on sophisticated literary elements such as theme, tone, and setting and on concepts such as symbolism, foreshadowing, and irony. By reading carefully selected children's literature, students can "see" the literary elements and discover the meanings behind the more difficult concepts that characterize higher-level reading.

> *By reading carefully selected children's literature, students can "see" the literary elements and discover the meanings behind the more difficult concepts that characterize higher-level reading.*

The bird in Eve Bunting's *Fly Away Home*, illustrated by Ronald Himler, serves as a symbol of the directionless flitting of the family who lives in an airport because they cannot afford rent or house payments. The young boy and his father, representing a newly defined "family" in society, live from day to day, trying to stay hidden in the hustle and bustle of people constantly on the move. A "little brown bird" trapped within the reflecting windows and cavernous spaces of the airport persistently tries to butt against the structure to find its way out of confinement. Also a symbol of resistance to the system causing or contributing to homelessness, the bird invites multileveled interpretations. Both the pictures and the text add richness to a high school reader's understanding of symbolism. They can enjoy clustering the meanings of the bird to help them interpret a subject that is difficult even for us experienced readers to understand: homelessness.

The following list includes other examples of children's books that can demonstrate the use of literary terms and make them more easily understandable for high school students.

Theme	*Dakota Dugout*, Ann Turner
	Richard Wright and the Library Card, William Miller
Setting	*When I Was Young in the Mountains*, Cynthia Rylant
	Moss Gown, William Hooks, illustrated by Donald Carrick
Tone	*A Visit to William Blake's Inn*, Nancy Willard (Compare Willard's version to Blake's *Songs of Innocence and Experience*.)
	The Tyger, William Blake, illustrated by Neil Waldman
Point of view	*Encounter*, Jane Yolen, illustrated by David Shannon
	Frog Prince Continued, Jon Scieszka, illustrated by Steve Johnson
	Foreshadowing Piggybook, Anthony Browne
	Golem, David Wisniewski
Irony	*The Necklace*, Guy de Maupassant, illustrated by Gary Kelley
Symbolism	*The Wall* and *Smoky Night*, Eve Bunting, illustrated by Ronald Himler and David Diaz respectively
	Tikvah Means Hope and *The Keeping Quilt*, Patricia Polacco

When looking for quick ways to introduce study topics, children's literature can be the "short, live, on-the-spot" example. Social topics addressed in Maurice Sendak's *We Are All in the Dumps with Jack and Guy: Two Nursery Rhymes with Pictures* (homelessness, political origins of rhymes) or in Jane Yolen's *Letting Swift River Go* (change in a town when it is covered over by a dam's reservoir) can be better appreciated by adolescents than by younger children. Acculturation and cultural influences of multicultural people are topics in Patricia Polacco's *The Keeping Quilt* (Russian Jews in America) and Pegi Deitz Shea's *The Whispering Cloth: A Refugee's Story* (the Hmong route from their homeland to the United States as captured on a story quilt). *Wilfred Gordon McDonald Partridge* by Mem Fox is an excellent choice when examining service-learning topics because it addresses relationships between young and old people and demonstrates how physical objects can trigger memories for all people.

Writing Style, Genre, and Conventions

Parody and satire were always difficult to point out to my high school students. They did not seem to "read" these concepts with much sophistication, and consequently their reading missed a potential richness. After looking at *Piggie Pie!* by Margie Palatini, however, students could easily see the connections to "Old MacDonald Had a Farm" and understand the concept of parody. A look at *The Book That Jack Wrote* reveals how Jon Scieszka parodies "The House That Jack Built." Students likewise can understand satire after they read *The Paper Bag Princess* by Robert Munsch or *Princess Furball* by Charlotte Huck, takeoffs and twisted versions of the Cinderella story. Both of these examples of satire also clearly model the use of stereotypes. Additional titles to examine for satire include David Macauley's *Baaa* (also good for allegory) or Nikolai Gogol's *The Nose.*

The story within a story, a writer's plot device used in more sophisticated books, looks simpler in *The Quicksand Book* by Tomie De Paola, *Zin! Zin! Zin! A Violin* by Lloyd Moss, or *Black and White* by David Macaulay. The convoluted four stories in *Black and White* are told through illustrations and very few words, and should lead to student insights regarding the story-within-a-story structure found in other works of literature and used extensively in media arts.

Examining the entire collection of works by individual authors can emphasize writers' different styles. I suggest the writings of prolific authors such as Robert D. San Souci, Eve Bunting, Paul Goble, Cynthia Rylant, Maurice Sendak, Ann Turner, or Kevin Henkes, for all have distinctive writing styles that model writing for specific audiences, with dialogue, in different genres, or for varying levels of understanding. San Souci models character relationships, patterns of folktales, and structural rules of traditional stories. Sendak uses old rhymes and exaggerated dreams as elements in his interpretations of modern social topics. Henkes's family relationships come through in art and word as characters skip across a page and change size. Goble uses similes and metaphors that reflect Native American ideas and customs.

Looking at different writers' versions of the same folktale, such as the Cinderella story, can demonstrate how a writer's style influences understandings of a story. I used *Yeh Shen: A Cinderella Story from China* (Ai-Ling Louie), *The Rough Faced Girl* (Rafe Martin), and *The Egyptian Cinderella* (Shirley Climo) to help students see the impact of writing style and cultural influences on interpretations of folktales. Martin's Algonquin telling of the fire-scarred girl who marries the Invisible

Being uses phrases and words that represent the Algonquin speech. Audience and perspective play important roles in the choice of words and references in the story. Comparing Martin's version with other ethnic stories encourages high school students to consider how point of view and projected audience affect a writer's style.

Before studying different characteristics of genres in their literature texts or in adult literature, students can learn to point out differences among the genres in children's literature. For traditional literature, *Seven Blind Mice* by Ed Young (East Indian fable), *The Girl Who Loved Wild Horses* by Paul Goble (Native American myth), and *Saint George and the Dragon* by Margaret Hodges (English legend) model the genre prototypes. For modern fantasy, I use *Verdi*, by Janell Cannon, about a snake whose feelings do matter; I also suggest *The Polar Express* by Chris Van Allsburg, a Christmas story for anyone who can still "believe" as children. For contemporary realistic fiction, almost anything by Eve Bunting, especially *Fly Away Home*, about homelessness, or *A Day's Work*, about the relationship between a Hispanic boy and his grandfather, demonstrates realism at its best. The characteristics of historical fiction are obvious in Patricia Polacco's *Pink and Say*, a poignant Civil War story, and Shulamith Levey Oppenheim's *The Lily Cupboard: A Story of the Holocaust*, about a Jewish girl hiding during World War II. All of these picture books exhibit the characteristics of the genres that help students distinguish between the genres through which authors of young adult and adult texts have chosen to present their messages and stories.

Succinct, Targeted Language

Because picture books must be short given the reading abilities of their target audience, children's authors imbue each word with multiple meanings. Mem Fox loads her words in *Wilfrid Gordon McDonald Partridge* with social connotations much more sophisticated than the young reader of the picture book could appreciate (see Figure 10.1). In *Wilfrid*, a young boy wants to help his ninety-year-old friend who lives in the old folks home next door regain her memory. When he asks several of the residents for a definition of a memory, they tell him that memories make you laugh or cry, are warm, may be from long ago, and are as precious as gold. Wilfrid collects all his special objects that meet these criteria and presents each of them to Miss Alison so she can remember her own special memories: a bird's nest, her brother who died in war, a walk with her sister on the beach, a puppet on strings,

Figure 10.1. Book Cover of *Wilfrid Gordon McDonald Partridge* by Mem Fox

and the day she met Wilfrid. Memories take on personal meanings that expand relative to the age of the reader. The book's depiction of the special relationship between the young and the old comes alive in the art and the text. This book lends itself to all types and ages of audiences because it is such a beautiful story told "by a small boy, who wasn't very old either" (Fox, 1989, unpaged).

Patricia McKissack uses speech patterns from ancient African language in *Mirandy and Brother Wind*, the story of a cakewalk in the rural South. Grandmamma Beasley calls Mirandy "chile" and describes

Brother Wind with "He be special. He be free" (McKissack, 1988, un-paged). When high school students read these lines, they understand why the dialect is so important to character development and how the language builds a background for the setting. Robert D. San Souci's *The Talking Eggs*, illustrated by Jerry Pinkney (a Cajun Cinderella story set in Louisiana), and Sherley Anne Williams's *Working Cotton*, illustrated by Carole Byard (the story of migrant workers in southern California cotton fields), model use of dialect in conversation while at the same time letting the words and illustrations define the setting and imagery. Chris Raschka uses one or two words per page, plus body language, for each boy's contributions to a conversation in *Yo! Yes?* The connotations in the inflections, the facial expressions, and the growth of friendship between an African American boy and his white friend deliver humor, social commentary, and rhythm, all with a hand-ful of words.

Picture book authors have to be sure that each word carries its full weight in connotations and implications, and that each word con-tributes to understandings of the text and interpretations of the illus-trations. For these reasons, some picture books contain levels of meaning far beyond casual first readings. High school students who try to create picture books for young students quickly appreciate the craft and art involved in writing for these young readers. When older students are paired with younger children, the specific needs of their audience help them respond in their own writing to word choice, syn-tax, and overall meaning. With the publication of their own picture books, they also can reflect on and practice the skills needed to read aloud to young children.

Reading for Specific Content Areas

Usually we look to informational or nonfiction books to present vocab-ulary, concepts, and connections that high school students need for all areas of the curriculum. But reading skills such as skimming, reading headings, examining first and last sentences in paragraphs, spotting unfamiliar words, going from general to specific concepts or vice versa, and pinpointing perspective or bias by identifying "hot" words are all skills students can practice using children's books, without being overwhelmed by longer texts. These same skills can then be transferred to newspapers, magazines, and reference tools, as well as the students' other textbooks.

The Magic School Bus series by Joanna Cole offers sophisticated science and mathematics concepts in picture book format. High school students examining these deceptively simple books can use their reading skills while looking for confirmation of content they know, explanations that can be easily understood, and concepts that reinforce their own understandings. Likewise, the *Greatest Newspaper in Civilization* series published by Candlewick Press offers entertaining looks at history, allowing students to practice their content-specific reading strategies. Each one of these newspaper books addresses a specific time period, civilization, and historical facts and theories of interpretations. Carmen Agra Deedy's *Agatha's Feather Bed: Not Just Another Wild Goose Story*, illustrated by Laura L. Seeley, is an excellent example of science and mathematics concepts in a modern fantasy book, full of puns and wordplay. Deedy illustrates how "something comes from something" and seeks the origins of many commonplace things. Pages are framed with quilt designs containing materials that themselves become objects to investigate, such as glass and diamonds, boar bristles and linen. Many other titles address specific topics and are usually recommended by the curriculum-area national organizations' publications.

Connecting Print and Illustrations

One of the earliest reading strategies young children learn is to "read" the pictures that accompany the text of a story. Picture books offer extra artistic clues for understanding literary elements, writers' styles, and curriculum-area content. Older students can take advantage of pictures in children's literature to practice predicting, comprehending, synthesizing, and evaluating. Children's books of poetry are especially helpful for demonstrating to students how they can use the art in picture books to help them apply higher-level thinking skills in reading. Joyce Carol Thomas's illustrations in her *Brown Honey in Broomwheat Tea*, and Alice Provensen and Martin Provensen's illustrations in Nancy Willard's *A Visit to William Blake's Inn: Poems for Innocent and Experienced Travelers*, as well as Douglas Florian's art in his book *In the Swim*, are excellent examples of how pictures can enhance the comprehension of poetry. Thomas uses tea-washed colors, impressionistic art, and beguiling little-girl features to demonstrate the innocence of an African American girl who learns to be proud of her skin color. The Provensens' typical gouache illustrations (watercolor with the addition of chalk to achieve an effect close to tempera), in the style and technique of William Blake's own time, detail characters in humorous situations. Florian's concrete poetry and watercolor illustrations humorously depict a fish theme while giving lifestyle information about aquatic creatures. Stephen Gammell illustrates American Indian lifestyles in Virginia Driving Hawk Sneve's *Dancing Teepees: Poems for American Indian Youth*, yet another poetry book in picture book format. This book also demonstrates the importance of oral history in Native American culture.

Literary Criticism Applied to Children's Literature

In high school, students may be expected to learn to read texts with an understanding of critical theory. Thankfully, reader-response theory has replaced the dogmatic interpretations of New Criticism so that texts are not limited to one correct interpretation or understanding. Once students get beyond a passive reading of literature, good readers can look at works from different interpretations or critical perspectives, from mythic and rhetorical to social and feminist.

In mythic criticism, readers look for archetypal patterns that define genre and narrative forms. Gerald McDermott's *Raven: A Trickster Tale from the Pacific Northwest* exemplifies a good picture book for examining mythic criticism. May (1995) explains that mythic criticism lets students isolate archetypal patterns for defining a text's meaning. This is sophisticated thinking for most high school students. Seeing how it works in a picture book helps students understand this concept.

Rhetorical criticism looks at the author's influence on the text of a book. Historical fiction especially can be examined with this critical eye since authors are presenting a specific interpretation of history. *When Jessie Came across the Sea* by Amy Hest, illustrated by P. J. Lynch, looks at early immigration to the United States with the goal of demonstrating how hope and courage can propel anyone who seeks a better life. A young Jewish girl is selected to come to the United States, where she uses her sewing talents developed by her grandmother to achieve the American dream. Through a particularly ironic female Jewish character from eastern Europe, Hest demonstrates the determination of immigrants to adjust and to achieve. Rhetorical criticism looks at how authors present their arguments for a particular conclusion or interpretation. Through Jessie's eyes, Hest contrasts an impersonal Ellis Island reception for new settlers with the love Jessie feels toward her grandmother, who eventually comes to the United States to attend Jessie's wedding. Cultural criticism may be considered a subset of rhetorical criticism. Examining how the language and illustrations of a picture book depict different cultural or ethnic groups helps students view a book from a specific perspective. To investigate how cultural voice and language influence readers, students might examine Joseph Bruchac and Jonathan London's *Thirteen Moons on Turtle's Back: A Native American Year of Moons*.

Social criticism can examine the social and moral messages found in some picture books. Eve Bunting, Lynn Cherry, and Jane Yolen often present books that have social and moral messages about the destruction of families by war (Bunting's *The Wall*), environmental issues (Cherry's *A River Ran Wild*), and interpretations of American history from a native's perspective (Yolen's *Encounter*). Ann Turner's *Dakota Dugout* is a complex picture book that implies values held by the early settlers in the U.S. West and that comments on the desolation and bleakness of the geography through its words as well as through the black-and-white art of Ronald Himler. From the first-person perspective, a woman remembers what she felt when she first saw her sod house on the Dakota prairie, her deep sorrow when winter killed the cattle and drought sizzled the crops, and her appreciation of the hardships of living with and despite nature. One moral of Turner's book is expressed in its last words: "Sometimes the things we start with are best" (1985, unpaged).

In a feminist interpretation, readers look at male and female characters in relation to their roles in society. For reading from a feminist theoretical perspective, Trina Schart Hyman's illustrations for retold folktales are excellent examples. Her artistic representations of *Snow White* (Heins, 1974) and *Little Red Riding Hood* project her personal interpretations of females in literature. Both main characters are strong, sensuous women who defy traditional folktale characteristics. Hyman uses color to set the mood for the stories, details the effects of jealousy in the face of the queen, and makes Little Red Riding Hood susceptible to the wolf because of her youth and innocence.

Literary criticism applied to picture books changes the reader's viewpoint. Before asking high school students to apply these theories to longer works, we would be wise to model their applications to children's literature. I have successfully had high school students examine the same book from different critical perspectives to determine if our own biases and understandings, as well as those of the author and the social times, can make a difference in their interpretations. Students also begin to experience how looking at books from different critical perspectives can enhance their own reading responses.

Connecting with High School Literature

All English teachers have experienced the dilemma of assigning a novel and three weeks later realizing that our students did not understand what was happening in the book. By using a picture book to introduce a topic, a theme, or a concept, we may alleviate some of that confusion. The list is long of children's books with thematic connections to classics usually read in the high school classroom. A few examples help demonstrate possible connections.

For presenting the plot of Shakespeare's *King Lear,* students might first read *Moss Gown* by William Hooks, a Cinderella-like story set in the Deep South. For the concepts of a futuristic society and fear of the unknown, the high school English teacher can pair Chris Van Allsburg's *Bad Day at Riverbend* with *The Giver* by Lois Lowry or *1984* by George Orwell. As an introduction to Thornton Wilder's *Our Town,* students could discuss perceptions of change in Jane Yolen's *Letting Swift River Go.* Certainly, pairing Patricia Polacco's *Pink and Say* with any Civil War novel read in high school would illicit wonderful parallels of themes and topics. Both Pink and Say are fully developed characters who share a fear but also a respect for the cause of the Civil War. The conclusion to Polacco's book is especially moving. For Robert Frost's poem "Stopping by Woods on a Snowy Evening," use the illustrated version by Susan Jeffers, or for Coleridge's "The Rime of the Ancient Mariner," use the illustrated picture book by Ed Young. Truman Capote's *A Christmas Story* and *The Thanksgiving Visitor* have been illustrated by Beth Peck, giving new meanings to the readings of these traditional stories. The layers of understanding in Twain's *The Adventures of Huckleberry Finn* can first be explored in David Macauley's *Black and White.*

Conclusion

Works of children's literature serve multiple purposes: they can be good pieces of literature and works of art, and they can be worthy of study and capable of entertaining and teaching. Thus, children's literature provides something of value to people of all ages, including high school students. Picture books offer familiar story formats and plots, nonthreatening sources for successful attempts at reading. The ways we introduce these picture books to older students will determine how well the students accept their presence in the high school classroom. Teachers who are excited about the medium and appreciate picture books as pieces of literature and who have a repertoire of classroom teaching techniques are the most likely to successfully incorporate this rich reading resource. Besides sitting in the children's sections of bookstores or libraries and reading and enjoying their selections, the best way to become familiar with picture books that are suitable for high school classrooms is to talk with elementary library media specialists or elementary classroom teachers. They will be glad to share their own love of picture books with those of us who don't usually "get" to read and appreciate children's literature.

References

Ammon, B. D., & Sherman, G. W. (1996). *Worth a thousand words: An annotated guide to picture books for older readers.* Englewood, CO: Libraries Unlimited.

Benedict, S., & Carlisle, L. (Eds.). (1992). *Beyond words: Picture books for older readers and writers.* Portsmouth, NH: Heinemann.

Blake, W. (1991). *Songs of innocence and of experience.* Princeton, NJ: William Blake Trust and Princeton University Press.

Blake, W. (1993). *The tyger* (N. Waldman, Illus.). San Diego, CA: Harcourt Brace.

Browne, A. (1986). *Piggybook.* New York: Knopf.

Bruchac, J., & London, J. (1992). *Thirteen moons on turtle's back: A native American year of moons* (T. Locker, Illus.). New York: Philomel Books.

Bunting, E. (1994). *A day's work* (R. Himler, Illus.). New York: Clarion Books.

Bunting, E. (1991). *Fly away home* (R. Himler, Illus.). New York: Clarion Books.

Bunting, E. (1994). *Smoky night* (D. Diaz, Illus.). San Diego, CA: Harcourt Brace.

Bunting, E. (1990). *The wall* (R. Himler, Illus.). New York: Clarion Books.

Cannon, J. (1997). *Verdi.* San Diego, CA: Harcourt Brace.

Capote, T. (1989). *A Christmas memory* (B. Peck, Illus.). New York: Knopf.

Capote, T. (1997). *The Thanksgiving visitor* (B. Peck, Illus.). New York: Scholastic.

Cherry, L. (1992). *A river ran wild: An environmental history.* San Diego, CA: Harcourt Brace Jovanovich.

Climo, S. (1992). *Egyptian Cinderella.* New York: Harper Trophy.

Cole, J. (1987). *The magic school bus: Inside the Earth* (B. Degen, Illus.). New York: Scholastic.

Coleridge, S. T. (1992). *The rime of the ancient mariner* (E. Young, Illus). New York: Atheneum.

Deedy, C. A. (1991). *Agatha's feather bed: Not just another wild goose story* (L. L. Seeley, Illus.). Atlanta, GA: Peachtree.

De Paola, T. (1977). *The quicksand book*. New York: Holiday House.

Florian, D. (1997). *In the swim: Poems and paintings*. San Diego, CA: Harcourt Brace.

Fox, M. (1989). *Wilfrid Gordon McDonald Partridge* (J. Vivas, Illus.). New York: Kane/Miller.

Frost, R. (1978). *Stopping by woods on a snowy evening* (S. Jeffers, Illus.). New York: Dutton.

Goble, P. (1986). *The girl who loved wild horses*. New York: Aladdin Books.

Gogol, N. (1993). *The nose* (G. Spirin, Illus.). Boston: Godine.

The greatest newspaper in civilization. (Series). Cambridge, MA: Candlewick Press.

Heins, P. (1974). *Snow White* (T. S. Hyman, Illus.). Boston: Little, Brown.

Herz, S. K., with Gallo, D. R. (1996). *From Hinton to Hamlet: Building bridges between young adult literature and the classics*. Westport, CT: Greenwood Press.

Hest, A. (1997). *When Jessie came across the sea* (P. J. Lynch, Illus.). Cambridge, MA: Candlewick Press.

Hodges, M. (1984). *Saint George and the dragon: A golden legend* (T. S. Hyman, Illus.). Boston: Little, Brown.

Hooks, W. (1987). *Moss gown* (D. Carrick, Illus.). New York: Clarion Books.

Huck, C. (1989). *Princess Furball* (A. Lobel, Illus.). New York: Greenwillow Books.

Hyman. T. S. (1983). *Little Red Riding Hood*. New York: Holiday House.

Kaywell, J. F. (Ed.). (1993). *Adolescent literature as a complement to the classics*. Norwood, MA: Christopher Gordon.

Kaywell, J. F. (Ed.). (1995). *Adolescent literature as a complement to the classics, Vol. 2*. Norwood, MA: Christopher Gordon.

Kaywell, J. F. (Ed.). (1997). *Adolescent literature as a complement to the classics, Vol. 3*. Norwood, MA: Christopher Gordon.

Kaywell, J. F. (Ed.). (2000). *Adolescent literature as a complement to the classics, Vol. 4*. Norwood, MA: Christopher Gordon.

Louie, A.-L. (1982). *Yeh-Shen: A Cinderella story from China*. New York: Philomel Books.

Lowry, L. (1993). *The giver*. Boston: Houghton Mifflin.

Macaulay, D. (1985). *Baaa*. Boston: Houghton Mifflin.

Macaulay, D. (1990). *Black and white*. Boston: Houghton Mifflin.

Martin, R. (1992). *The rough faced girl*. New York: Putnam.

Maupassant, G. de. (1993). *The necklace* (G. Kelley, Illus.). Mankato, MN: Creative Editions.

May, J. P. (1995). *Children's literature and critical theory: Reading and writing for understanding*. New York: Oxford University Press.

McDermott, G. (1993). *Raven: A trickster tale from the Pacific Northwest*. San Diego, CA: Harcourt Brace.

McKissack, P. (1988). *Mirandy and Brother Wind* (Jerry Pinkney, Illus.). New York: Knopf.

Miller, W. (1997). *Richard Wright and the library card*. New York: Lee & Low Books.

Moss, L. (1995). *Zin! Zin! Zin! A violin* (M. Priceman, Illus.). New York: Scholastic.

Munsch, R. (1980). *The paper bag princess*. Toronto: Annick Press.

Norton, D. E., with Norton, S. E. (1999). *Through the eyes of a child: An introduction to children's literature* (5th ed.). Upper Saddle River, NJ: Merrill.

Oppenheim, S. L. (1992). *The lily cupboard: A story of the Holocaust* (R. Himler, Illus.). New York: HarperCollins.

Orwell, G. (1950). *1984*. New York: Signet Classic/Penguin.

Palatini, M. (1995). *Piggie Pie!* (H. Fine, Illus.). New York: Clarion Books.

Pirie, B. (1997). *Reshaping high school English*. Urbana, IL: National Council of Teachers of English.

Polacco, P. (1998). *The keeping quilt*. New York: Simon & Schuster.

Polacco, P. (1994). *Pink and say*. New York: Philomel Books.

Polacco, P. (1994). *Tikvah means hope*. New York: Doubleday.

Raschka, C. (1993). *Yo! Yes?* New York: Orchard Books.

Rylant, C. (1985). *When I was young in the mountains* (D. Goode, Illus.). New York: Dutton.

San Souci, R. D. (1989). *The talking eggs: A folktale from the American South* (J. Pinkney, Illus.). New York: Dial Books.

Scieszka, J. (1994). *The book that Jack wrote* (D. Adel, Illus.). New York: Viking.

Scieszka, J. (1991). *Frog prince continued* (S. Johnson, Illus.). New York: Viking.

Sendak, M. (1993). *We are all in the dumps with Jack and Guy: Two nursery rhymes with pictures*. New York: HarperCollins.

Shakespeare, W. (1997). *King Lear* (R. A. Foakes, Ed., 3rd ed.). London: Thomas Nelson and Sons.

Shea, P. D. (1995). *The whispering cloth: A refugee's story*. Honesdale, PA: Boyds Mills Press.

Shively, J. (1993). Picture books? In middle school and high school? *Connecticut English Journal*, *22*, 30–33.

Sneve, V. D. H. (1989). *Dancing teepees: Poems of American Indian youth* (S. Gammell, Illus.). New York: Holiday House.

Thomas, J. C. (1993). *Brown honey in broomwheat tea* (F. Cooper, Illus.). New York: HarperCollins.

Turner, A. (1985). *Dakota dugout* (R. Himler, Illus.). New York: Macmillan.

Twain, M. (1996). *The adventures of Huckleberry Finn.* New York: Oxford University Press.

Van Allsburg, C. (1995). *Bad day at Riverbend.* Boston: Houghton Mifflin.

Van Allsburg, C. (1985). *The polar express.* Boston: Houghton Mifflin.

Wilder, T. (1998). *Our town.* New York: Perennial Classics.

Willard, N. (1981). *A visit to William Blake's inn: Poems for innocent and experienced travelers* (A. Provensen & M. Provensen, Illus.). New York: Harcourt Brace Jovanovich.

Williams, S. A. (1992). *Working cotton* (C. M. Byard, Illus.). San Diego, CA: Harcourt Brace Jovanovich.

Wisniewski, D. (1996). *Golem.* New York: Clarion Books.

Yolen, J. (1992). *Encounter* (D. Shannon, Illus.). San Diego, CA: Harcourt Brace Jovanovich.

Yolen, J. (1992). *Letting swift river go.* Boston: Little, Brown.

Young, E. (1992). *Seven blind mice.* New York: Philomel Books.

Afterword: Future Directions for Reading in High School

Leila Christenbury
Virginia Commonwealth University

Alberto Manguel's *A History of Reading* (1996) provides insight into that most powerful of human activities, reading, an activity that Manguel notes began around 4,000 B.C. with a clay tablet inscription. Since that time, reading has expanded exponentially across the world, and while Manguel notes that today about a quarter of the world's population cannot read, just recently almost 360,000 books were added in a single year to the Library of Congress's current collection of 100 million books. Beyond the facts and figures and dates, however, *A History of Reading* acutely observes the social and psychological aspects of reading:

> In every literate society, learning to read is something of an initiation, a ritualized passage out of a state of dependency and rudimentary communication. The child learning to read is admitted into the communal memory by way of books, and thereby becomes acquainted with a common past which he or she renews, to a greater or lesser degree, in every reading. (p. 71)

This link to a shared past, this membership in a community memory, is certainly central to the power and pleasure of being a reader. And for me, although I may be optimistic, I see the future of reading as a bright one. I can barely find a space for my car in the parking lots of my city's mega-bookstores—and it is my impression that not everyone inside those buildings is just sipping double decaf lattes and shopping for alternative rock CDs. I see in those bookstores serious buying and reading going on, and when folks leave those buildings, they leave with bags of books and magazines in hand.

In my personal life, I am regularly asked by friends and acquaintances for book recommendations, and not all of those who ask are teachers or academics. Many of my friends work outside the schools—one, for instance, works in a printing plant, one is a master welder, and one is a graphic designer—and all three in the past few months have asked me for titles of good books to read. It seems that more folks than just English teachers are going to bed not with the remote control in hand, but with a new book.

Another cause for optimism is the unexpected boost reading receives from television and the Internet. Spinning through the many available TV channels, literary talk shows are regularly showcased on cable stations, and publishers, authors, and readers take up airtime talking about books and reading. This extends to the Internet: I have yet to meet someone who hasn't at least heard of—if not ordered from—one of the most accessible bookstores on earth, amazon.com. In addition, full-text articles and parts of books are now widely available electronically. Today, our televisions and our computers do not so much compete as help support and extend reading.

So, from my perspective, it appears that reading as a widespread social and recreational activity is more alive and well than many might assume. To me, at least, reading does not seem currently endangered because my evidence tells me that many folks are reading and reading regularly.

But what I am describing is reading at large, reading outside the schools—reading, as it were, in the wild. Sadly, reading in school, specifically high school, is a different matter, and there, in my judgment, much silliness and even hypocrisy persist. Therefore, I do not view the future of reading in high school as optimistically as I see the future of reading in general, and I think we must do something about that. Right now.

It pains me to write this, but in high school much of our good sense about what readers need and who readers are evaporates. In high school, we pay lip service to reading as an important activity, but we rarely make time for it in the school day, leaving our students with the unmistakable impression that reading is not important enough to occupy any part of their instructional time. It is surely clear to our students that we can make room within the school day for testing and counseling and yearbook pictures and even award assemblies and pep rallies, but allowing a student to pick up a book or a magazine for a sustained period in an academic class is somehow wasting time. Letting students read *in* school should be one of our priorities; it reinforces for students—and it reminds us as educators—that reading is as valuable an instructional activity as any we can devise.

In high school, we also rarely talk about reading with our students as though it is a significant part of our adult lives. Thus, reading seems to be an activity far below the stature of the latest sporting event we attended, the last movie we saw, or the last trip we took, topics that many teachers regularly share with their students. If reading in school were a common or even omnipresent activity, and if we, as teachers and adults, behaved as though reading were important in our lives, perhaps we would feel more comfortable talking with our students about reading in general and our own reading in particular.

Further, in school, particularly in English class, we often act as though reading involves only one kind of legitimate printed matter—all else does not qualify. In this way, we jettison much nonfiction and almost all technical works; we scorn the contemporary and even the pop as if they are not real reading, certainly not worthy of our time. Inadvertently, or sometimes directly, we tell our students that reading is only Keats or Austen or Morrison, never *Sports Illustrated* or Stephen King or *Chicken Soup for the Teenage Soul.* We thus tell students that the reading world is a very small one with fairly rigid boundaries. This is not encouraging or inviting, and many of our students accordingly decline to enter that little, circumscribed country of what we narrowly define as reading.

Finally, in high school the major way we credit reading is through testing and, even worse, through recall testing: What was the name of the man she met? When did the neighbor find the dog's body? What time did the clock chime? It appears that in school, reading is often just another reason for the teacher to make a mark in a grade book. Also, frequently the students' only postreading activity is fact-oriented testing. This is, without a doubt, a depressing and narrow way to judge and to credit student reading, and it stifles one of the great pleasures of reading—discussing and sharing ideas with other readers and exploring more than the minutiae of plot details.

This picture does not bode well for the future of reading in high school, a future which can certainly be brighter, I think, if we can all agree

- that reading is an important enough activity to be pursued within the school day
- that we teachers too are readers and should talk with our students about our reading
- that our students should be encouraged to see reading as wide ranging and omnivorous, not confined to a single genre such as fiction or poetry, or to established, classic authors

- that we can do much more after reading than administer a test that, in many cases, measures only how many factual plot details students can recall

In the foreword of this book, John Mayher writes eloquently of living on the planet of readers, of inviting our students to read joyfully and voluntarily and to respond to the call of stories. The writers of the body of this volume offer ideas, strategies, and approaches to ensure this kind of response. For my part, I offer my own ideas about students and reading and what we as teachers can do to further what is no less than a great enterprise. Certainly I can conclude this brief afterword with my own testimonial: Reading has been utterly central to my life. It has informed, instructed, and inspired; it has taken me away when I needed to leave and has brought me back when I needed to return. If it were not for reading, my life, in almost all its aspects, would be painted in shades of gray.

As a teacher, as a reader, I look for the day when all of my students see reading similarly—as an adventure and a joy, as the non-negotiable centerpiece of a good life, and, as Manguel maintains, as an entrance ticket into our common past. I believe that goal can be achieved. If we rethink our attitude and refigure what we currently do in our classrooms, the future of reading in high school can be very bright indeed.

Reference

Manguel, A. (1996). *A history of reading.* New York: Viking.

Editor

Bonnie O. Ericson currently serves as chair of the Department of Secondary Education at California State University, Northridge, where she has regularly taught methods of teaching English and content-area literacy courses. She has served on the NCTE Secondary Section Committee, and for four years edited the Resources and Reviews column for *English Journal.*

Contributors

Janet S. Allen is an international consultant recognized for her literacy work with at-risk students. She is the author of *It's Never Too Late: Leading Adolescents to Lifelong Literacy* and *Words, Words, Words: Teaching Vocabulary in Grades 4–12*, and coauthor of *There's Room for Me Here: Literacy Workshop in the Middle School*. Her latest book is *Yellow Brick Roads: Shared and Guided Paths to Independent Reading*. Allen has also written several articles and chapters related to young adult literature and teaching. She taught high school reading and English in northern Maine until 1992 when she relocated to Florida to teach English and reading courses at the University of Central Florida. During her tenure at UCF, she directed the Central Florida Writing Project and assisted in the creation of the Orange County Literacy Project. Allen has received numerous teaching awards including the Milken Foundation's National Educator Award. She recently resigned her position at the university and is currently researching, writing, speaking, and conducting literacy institutes across the country.

Jeannie Beckett is the Title I coordinator at Anaheim High School in California. She serves on the district Language Arts Task Force and is a district trainer for content-area teachers in the use of informal reading inventories.

Lois Buckman has been a librarian with the Conroe Independent School District for the past seven years. She is currently the lead librarian at Moorhead/Caney Creek Academic Complex. Prior to that, Lois taught English language arts to middle-level students for twenty-five years, first in New Jersey, then in Texas. Because she is in the unique position of serving both junior high and high school, she is able to follow the reading habits of students for five years, enabling her to determine what they like to read as they mature.

Leila Christenbury is a former high school English teacher who is currently professor of English education at Virginia Commonwealth University in Richmond. A former editor of *English Journal*, she is the president-elect of NCTE. Christenbury is the author of numerous books, including *Making the Journey: Being and Becoming a Teacher of English Language Arts* and *Both Art and Craft: Teaching Ideas That Spark Learning* (with Diana Mitchell), as well as chapters and articles on the teaching of English. She is a regular speaker across the country on issues of methodology, reading, and materials selection for the secondary classroom.

Sandra Okura DaLie teaches at Ulysses S. Grant School in Valley Glen, California. In addition to teaching high school English, she is a part-time instructor at California State University, Northridge, teaching reading methods courses and supervising student teachers in English. She frequently serves as a consultant for the education department of the Japanese American National Museum.

Linda L. Flammer began her teaching career in 1979. She currently teaches English in the Math, Science, and Technology Magnet School at John H. Francis Polytechnic High School in Sun Valley, California. Her current teaching assignment includes American literature, composition, and literary analysis. Flammer earned her master's degree in secondary education with an emphasis in English education from California State University, Northridge, in 1999. In addition to her regular teaching assignments, she has served as mentor teacher for the Los Angeles Unified School District and a teacher trainer for California State University, Northridge. Flammer specializes in literacy instruction for at-risk adolescents.

John Gaughan has been teaching English at Lockland High School near Cincinnati, Ohio, for nineteen years. He has been associated with the Ohio Writing Project since 1983 and has presented papers at the NCTE Annual Convention and the NCTE Spring Conference. He has published articles in *English Journal, English Education,* and *Voices from the Middle,* and is the author of *Cultural Reflections: Critical Teaching and Learning in the English Classroom* and *Reinventing English: Teaching in the Contact Zone.* He enjoys golfing and coaching his daughters' soccer and basketball teams.

Lupe Gutierrez is chair of the Department of English Language Development at Anaheim High School in California. She participates in district curriculum development and has taught English classes for parents of Anaheim students.

Teri S. Lesesne is associate professor in the Department of Library Science at Sam Houston State University, where she teaches classes in children's and young adult literature. A former middle school English teacher, Teri has been teaching at the university for eleven years. She is past president of the Texas Council of Teachers of English and the Greater Houston Area Reading Council. She is president of the Assembly on Literature for Adolescents of the National Council of Teachers of English (ALAN) and is the coeditor of the fourteenth edition of *Books for You* (with Kylene Beers). Lesesne writes the YA literature review column for *Voices from the Middle,* an author interview column for *Teacher Librarian,* and the children's review column for *The Journal of Children's Literature.*

Carolyn Lott, associate professor in curriculum and instruction at the University of Montana in Missoula, taught English and library science at the high school and middle school levels for nineteen years before moving to higher education to teach library science, children's and young adult literature, and curriculum classes. She served on NCTE's Executive Committee as chair of the Secondary Section Steering Committee, chaired SCOA, still works with Montana's NCTE affiliate, serves on the editorial board for *Knowledge Quest*, and is involved with inservice programs for literature and writing across the curriculum as well as information literacy skills.

John S. Mayher is professor of English education in the Department of Teaching and Learning at New York University, where he directs the teacher education program. A former junior and senior high school teacher, he now helps prospective teachers struggle with improving the literacy abilities of their students. His book *Uncommon Sense: Theoretical Practice in Language Education* won the Russell Award for Distinguished Research in the Teaching of English in 1991, and he was awarded the Distinguished Service Award by NCTE in 1998.

Jeff McQuillan is currently associate professor of education at California State University, Fullerton. His most recent book is *The Literacy Crisis: False Claims, Real Solutions*.

Matthew Rippon teaches English and reading at Anaheim High School in California. He is an adviser to the school's Student Coalition.

Susan Schauwecker teaches twelfth-grade English and Advanced Placement literature classes at McLane High School in Fresno, California, where her students are predominantly from inner-city migrant families from all over the world. She has taught English for nine years and been department chair for five. She is an active member of the California Association of Teachers of English (CATE) and the San Joaquin Valley Writing Project, and has been the NCTE Promising Young Writer's writing contest coordinator in California. Schauwecker is an advocate for language-acquisition students in the Fresno Unified School District and the California Department of Education. Her chapter comes from one of her presentations to CATE in Burbank, California.

Sue Snyder teaches English and English language development at Anaheim High School in California. She was elected to the School Site Council and serves on the Teacher Recognition Committee.

Lois T. Stover is professor and chair of educational studies at St. Mary's College of Maryland, where she supervises student teachers and teaches secondary methods classes, children's and young adult literature, and educational psychology. Coeditor of the thirteenth edition of *Books for You* and author of *Young Adult Literature: The Heart of the Middle School Curriculum*, Stover has also written articles for *English Journal* and *The ALAN Review*, and served as president of ALAN. She has also been a senior and middle school teacher of English and drama.

Doug Wager teaches English and reading at Anaheim High School in California. He is a technology coach through Anaheim's Digital High School program.

Gregg Williams teaches English and English language development at Anaheim High School . He works closely with the California State University, Fullerton, Black Mentor Program for Student Success.

Eydie Zajec teaches English and reading at Anaheim High School in California. She works with student teachers at California State University, Fullerton.

This book was set in Palatino and Helvetica by Precision Graphics.
The typeface used on the cover is Times.
This book was printed on 60-lb. Williamsburg Offset paper by Versa Press.